Toscanini

AN INTIMATE PORTRAIT

Da Capo Press Music Reprint Series

GENERAL EDITOR

FRANK D'ACCONE
University of California at Los Angeles

Toscanini

AN INTIMATE PORTRAIT

by

Samuel Chotzinoff

DA CAPO PRESS • NEW YORK • 1976

Library of Congress Cataloging in Publication Data

Chotzinoff, Samuel, 1889-1964.
  Toscanini: an intimate portrait.

  (Da Capo Press music reprint series)
  Reprint of the 1956 ed. published by Knopf, New York.
  1. Toscanini, Arturo, 1867-1957.
  [ML422.T67C38 1976]   785'.092'4 [B]   76-7576
  ISBN 0-306-70777-2

This Da Capo Press edition of *Toscanini: An Intimate Portrait* is an unabridged repub-
lication of the first edition published in New York in 1956. It is reprinted with the
permission of Alfred A. Knopf, Inc.

Published by Da Capo Press, Inc.
A Subsidiary of Plenum Publishing Corporation
227 West 17th Street, New York, N. Y. 10011

Manufactured in the United States of America

BY SAMUEL CHOTZINOFF

Toscanini: An Intimate Portrait (1956)

A Lost Paradise: Early Reminiscences (1955)

THESE ARE BORZOI BOOKS
PUBLISHED BY ALFRED A. KNOPF IN NEW YORK

TOSCANINI: *An Intimate Portrait*

Toscanini

AN INTIMATE PORTRAIT

by Samuel Chotzinoff

ALFRED A. KNOPF, NEW YORK

1956

All of the photographs in this book are by
Adrian Siegel
except for the outdoor snapshot
taken by the author

L. C. CATALOG CARD NUMBER: 56–5784

© *The Curtis Publishing Company, 1955; Samuel Chotzinoff, 1956.*

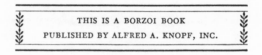

THIS IS A BORZOI BOOK
PUBLISHED BY ALFRED A. KNOPF, INC.

FIRST EDITION

The first four parts of this book originally appeared in HOLIDAY *in slightly different form.*

For Harry Sions, gratefully

TOSCANINI: *An Intimate Portrait*

CHAPTER ONE

𝒯HE first time I met Arturo Toscanini was in the spring of 1926. I was then music critic for the *New York World*, and I had been sent to Europe to report on musical events. In Paris, one day, I received a cablegram from my editor, Herbert Bayard Swope, telling me to go to Milan to investigate reported trouble between Toscanini and the Fascists. Rumors had reached New York that Toscanini had refused to open his performances at La Scala with the Fascist hymn and had severed his connection with the Milan opera house.

Knowing Toscanini's distaste for newspapermen, I took the precaution of obtaining a letter of introduction from a friend of his in New York. This letter, wrapped in a hundred-lire note, I presented to the concierge at Via Durini 20, the Maestro's seventeenth-century house in the heart of Milan. I was shown into a music room furnished in Victorian style, hung with many Victorian paintings in elaborate gilt frames, and adorned further with bronze figures of Verdi, Puccini, and Catalani; in black boxes, under glass, I saw plaster death masks of Beethoven and Verdi. The Maestro came in after a few minutes, shook my hand warmly, and motioned me to a chair. He was smartly dressed. Though the day was hot, he wore a vest, a starched shirt and wing collar; starched cuffs protruded from the sleeves of his black morning coat. His pants were striped, and his small shoes were newly shined. His sparse, soft white hair was brushed up at the sides, giving him the look of a satyr. His pepper-and-salt mustache was neatly trimmed, with both ends sticking up in points. His face was richly sunburned; although he was almost sixty, there was not a wrinkle on it. Fearing that I might never again have a chance to see him at such close range, I boldly scanned his face and figure. I was struck by the classic mold of his head, the beauty of his face, the dark intensity of his eyes; his look was so piercing that his eyes seemed to shoot out actual rays. I knew I was in the presence of a great man.

I told him frankly the purpose of my visit. He replied with a stream of Italian which I could not understand. A servant brought in coffee and poured two demi-tasses. I took a teaspoonful of sugar; the Maestro took four. We drank in silence. I began again, speaking slowly and in a kind of pidgin English that I hoped he would be able to grasp. I said I did not wish to pry into his affairs, but that his resistance to Fascism was of great concern to the world. My paper would like to have the privilege of presenting his side of the story, and so on. As I spoke I felt from the perplexed expression on his face that he did not understand a word. When I finished he stared intently at me for a while, and then looked away with the helpless air of a man who had tried his best to comprehend and could do no more. "I see," I said sadly, "you don't understand English." He nodded. Defeated, I rose to go. We shook hands. He saw me out politely, and as I descended the stairs he called out: "See Smeeze." I stopped and turned around, expecting him to say more. But no elucidation followed. "See Smeeze, see Smeeze," he reiterated, and I walked down the Via Durini repeating the cryptic words in an effort to arrive at their meaning.

Near the Scala I ran into Max Smith, the music critic on the *New York American*. Max was the only newspaperman Toscanini could tolerate, and Max in turn was extremely devoted to Toscanini; for him the Maestro was the world's only musical saint, and he, Max, was his self-confessed acolyte. He followed the Maestro wherever he went and kept voluminous notes on his performances, even to the metronomic timings of every piece of music he played, all for the benefit, presumably, of posterity. I was therefore not at all surprised to find Max in Milan.

Max spoke Italian well. I told him about my visit in the Via Durini and asked him if he could make anything out of the Maestro's advice or admonition or whatever the strange words implied. Max laughed and said it was plain enough: " 'See Smeeze' meant 'See Smith.' He was merely referring you to me for information about the La Scala situation."

"But doesn't Toscanini speak any English?" I asked. "After all, he spent seven winters in New York, from 1908 to 1915." Max blushed and turned the subject to the Maestro's present difficulties with the Milan Fascists. It then dawned on me that I had been the victim of the Maestro's extraordinary histrionic powers. Unwilling to discuss his troubles with me, he had pretended he could neither speak nor understand English. He had carried this out with the finesse of a great actor. And to dramatize his ignorance of the language and at the same time to show his willingness to be helpful, he had cannily referred me to his diplomatic acolyte. I could see that Italy had lost a star actor when Toscanini took up the baton.

That winter Toscanini was back in New York conducting the Philharmonic Symphony. I went to see him in the green room of Carnegie Hall after his first concert. I was amused to hear him speak beautiful, if archaic, English. And when I asked why he had misled me in Milan, he replied that he had never in his life given an interview to a newspaperman, and never would. Then, with a mischievous twinkle he added: "But you believed me, absolutely, no?" I told him that he was a wonderful actor and that he had had me fooled, absolutely! He looked very pleased.

I haunted the green room of Carnegie Hall after

every Toscanini concert. Though I was entitled, as a music critic, to a pair of seats, I subscribed to a second-tier box, one practically over the stage, from which I could see the conductor at very close range. For Toscanini had cast his spell over me, as he did over everyone who had access to him. Yet seeing him at close range did nothing to explain the mystery of his power. He did not, in fact, *exercise* power. He *radiated* it, effortlessly, unconsciously, like some absolute monarch of a long, unbroken, unopposed line of absolute monarchs. Nor could familiarity reveal the secret of his personal fascination. There was no one in any way like him, no one to whom I could compare him.

He was (and is) a law unto himself. I have never heard anyone seriously oppose him to his face on any subject whatsoever. One could disagree only silently, for open opposition might risk the most unpleasant of penalties—ostracism. To be shut out from that most exciting, that most exhilarating, personality was a dismaying deprivation. Of course no one would dare question his musical judgments. His knowledge of music was encyclopedic, his opinions solidly founded and therefore irrefutable. His talk on music was not academic. He did not regard music as an end in itself. It was for him a humane art, valid only when it expressed the heart or soul of man. That was why he distrusted purely contrapuntal musical forms. He often quoted Verdi on that very subject. He mistrusted the fugue, except for a few rare instances of what he called "human" fugues like the finale of Beethoven's String Quartet in C Major, Op. 59, and the finish of Verdi's *Falstaff*.

He loved certain Italian music so extravagantly as to make one suspect a tinge of chauvinism. And he was very proud of Scarlatti, Rossini, Verdi, Donizetti, Bellini, and his great friend Catalani. "Only an Italian could have written such music," he said. "Not Beethoven, not Weber, not Wagner, no . . . no . . . and no!" But, though the sincerity of his admiration for his countrymen was beyond question, his protestations were not without overtones of envy. As an Italian, he envied, secretly, the "cold" Teutonic countries their great musical figures of the past. However, his standard for Italian music was very high, except in certain instances when a personal bias made him endow a friend with the highest creative qualities.

Toscanini has always maintained that he has never permitted personal relationship to affect his musical judgments. Yet there is some evidence to the contrary. There is, for example, the music of his countryman, teacher, and friend Giuseppe Martucci. When Toscanini was young, Martucci was one of the first conductors to champion the music of Wagner and Brahms in Italy. Martucci was a very serious man, lofty in character and personally unassuming. Toscanini loved him unreservedly, so much so that he failed to perceive that Martucci's own compositions were unoriginal and showed a variety of influences, particularly that of Brahms. The fact that the public did not take to

Martucci's music saddened Toscanini, but made him more determined to play it. Wherever he went to conduct, Toscanini relentlessly played a symphony or concerto of Martucci. Toscanini's own family did not share his enthusiasm for his old teacher's music. They dreaded, like any audience, having to sit through a long composition that sounded like Brahms yet wasn't. But they dared not say so. However, they would warn me (as NBC's musical director) that the Maestro intended to play a Martucci composition, hoping that I might discover some way to avert what all of us considered rather a disaster. And one year, following such a warning, I tried what I thought was a subtle insinuation of my own distaste for Martucci. "Maestro," I said with an air of innocence, "does Martucci ever remind you of Brahms?" The Maestro regarded me wonderingly. "Never!" he snapped. And Martucci's Second Symphony duly appeared on one of his programs.

The Maestro not only adored Martucci's music; he also revered him as a man. The Maestro remembered even Martucci's wife as a paragon of what a conductor's helpmate ought to be. Mrs. Toscanini generally accompanied her husband to rehearsals, unpacked his valise, set out his things, and acted as valet; but the moment he left the green room for the stage she would go out shopping, returning in time to help him change his undershirt and alpaca rehearsal coat at intermission. Once when she was late in returning the Maestro said witheringly: "Martucci's wife was *always* around. She

9

never left his dressing room for a moment. *Mai—Mai* [never, never]!"

While Toscanini knew everything there was to know about music and could give any musicologist and theoretician cards and spades on the subjects of harmony, counterpoint, musical form, and musical history, his peasant intuition and levelheadedness had, like Verdi's, steered him clear of the lofty tomfoolery that makes some excellent musicians forget the primary objective of music—namely, the expression of emotion through song. The admonition *"canta"* (sing) was always on his lips. *"Canta!"* he forever implored or shouted at orchestras and singers, and he hunted the melody in a composition relentlessly, like a hunter stalking his prey. The architecture of music as exemplified in the symphonic form was, for him, a structure of melodic fabrics. A symphony, from a simple melodic one by Haydn or Mozart to one as complex as Sibelius's Fourth, was a continuous song. Even great composers sometimes unwittingly bury melodic continuity under layers of secondary sound; Toscanini would keep these secondary matters down to a level that permitted the melody to flow unimpeded. At the same time, his patrician abhorrence of sentimentality kept him from adding meretricious luster or passion to melody, whether in symphony or opera. That was why critics and intellectual dilettantes called his interpretation of Teutonic symphonic music "Italianate," and his interpretation of Italian opera "Germanic."

In the late twenties, when he was musical director of the New York Philharmonic Symphony, Toscanini lived in a modest suite at the Astor Hotel. A large advertising sign twinkled perpetually outside his living-room window. It did not disturb him in the least. On the contrary, he liked to watch it. He also enjoyed the crowds and the bustle in the lobbies of the hotel and the din of the surrounding Times Square area. In a narrow brownstone house connecting with the hotel lived his friends Fred and Elsa Muschenheim, proprietors of the Astor. The Muschenheims loved music and adored musicians, and gave large suppers for visiting and resident artists. The suppers for Toscanini were very special occasions because of the risk they entailed. Suppers for other musical celebrities held no risk whatsoever. There was rarely any possibility that the guest of honor, no matter how celebrated, would not show up. Nor was there any difficulty about whom to invite with the guest of honor. Not so with Toscanini.

In the first place, it had to be ascertained what Toscanini thought of the guests the Muschenheims proposed to invite. The Maestro had the most definite likes and dislikes. These, however, fluctuated unaccountably. He might look with disfavor today on a person he had cherished only yesterday. It was essential to check with him or his family or his friends. Furthermore, the Maestro held to a rigid code of behavior and morals, the test of which even members of his family and his intimate friends had to meet or suffer ostracism. For example, he frowned on divorce. While he cheerfully pointed out that marital fidelity was unnatural to man, he insisted that the legal bonds of matrimony were inviolable. A man might have many mistresses, but he could have only one wife. Those of his friends who contemplated divorce had to take into account the loss of his friendship. The Maestro also disapproved of remarriage after the death of a husband or wife, though he might forget his disapproval if the second marriage occurred after a respectable interval of several years. Any shorter period earned his displeasure and inspired swift retaliation. He struck back at one of his closest friends who married again only *one* year after his wife's demise. Notwithstanding their previous intimate association, the Maestro never again saw or spoke to the man. Thus, anyone desiring to entertain Toscanini was obliged to be informed on the up-to-the-minute status of the Maestro's friends.

In the second place, the Maestro's acceptance of an invitation was no guarantee of his attendance, especially on nights when he was conducting. Everything depended on how the concert (or opera) went. He might drive up to the stage entrance of Carnegie Hall at eight p.m. (he was the soul of promptness) in the best of spirits and three hours later leave it in black despair. There could then be no question of supper. The Maestro went straight to his bedroom at the Astor, where, crying imprecations at his orchestra or at himself, or both, he finally went exhausted and supperless to bed. Once, in Milan, after he conducted an opera at La Scala, he returned dejectedly to his home, where the table was set for the usual delayed dinner. As the members of his family made for the dining-room, he placed himself in front of the door and barred their entrance with planted feet and outstretched arms. "What!" he raged, "you can *eat* after such a performance! Shame on you. . . . Shame!" And the family perforce went hungry to bed.

The Muschenheims were Philharmonic Symphony subscribers and attended all of the Maestro's concerts. But not until they heard the very last note of a concert could they be certain he would grace their board a half-hour later. The hazards were many—an orchestral mishap, ill-timed applause, the reluctance of the soloist of the evening to take a bow alone, anything at all. One bitter February evening the Muschenheims left Carnegie Hall secure in the belief that everything was all right, that nothing had occurred to prevent the Maestro from coming to their house for supper as he had promised. They left, alas, a moment too soon. As the Maestro was taking his final bow an overenthusiastic admirer advanced to the stage and placed a floral wreath at the conductor's feet. Quite unaware that his hero associated floral offerings with mortuary rites, the donor was hardly prepared for his idol's strange reaction to his gift. Seeing the wreath, the Maestro blanched, stood irresolute for a moment, then turned tail and fled. Once clear of the stage he did not, as usual, proceed to his dressing-room to

change his sweat-drenched undershirt. Instead he ran
to the stage-door exit, scampered down the steps two at
a time, gained the street, and turned to Seventh Avenue,
down which he fled at top speed, followed by Bruno
Zirato, the Philharmonic manager, who had tried to
intercept his flight and now, winded and distraught,
limped helplessly far behind him. Bareheaded, his
starched shirt and collar wilted, the frock-coated conductor pushed his way nimbly through the crowds in
Times Square, gained his hotel, and shut himself in his
room for the night. At the same moment the unsuspecting Muschenheims were greeting their guests. Their
butler, holding a tray with a glass and a bottle of wine,
stood at the living-room door waiting for Toscanini. (On
arrival the Maestro usually declared he was "thirty"
(thirsty), and a glass of champagne was always ready
for him to put him in a genial humor and thus ease the
tension of the other guests.) On this night, however, the
tension was eased by a phone call from Mrs. Toscanini
saying the Maestro would not be down. Supper was
served, conversation was animated and uninhibited.
There were several musical "lions" among the guests.
But there was a noticeable want of glamour.

On those fortunate evenings when nothing untoward happened at Carnegie Hall and the Maestro did arrive, the Muschenheim abode seemed—to this guest, at
any rate—the most exciting place in the world. Aside
from the Maestro, one might find oneself seated at table
next to Fritz Kreisler, Jascha Heifetz, Vladimir Horowitz,

Lotte Lehmann, or some other world-famous artist. The Maestro was, of course, the focal point, and his presence affected all the other guests, both great and near-great. No one disputed his supremacy and no one ever seriously challenged his views, whether on music or on affairs in general. Mrs. Toscanini might sometimes say quietly but dogmatically: "*No, Papá, non è vero!*" and the atmosphere for a while would grow tense. But by and large the Maestro held forth without interruption.

His opinions of men and events were positive to a degree. Such-and-such an occurrence was a "*scandalo,*" or else, on the contrary, "*una meraviglia.*" This or that woman was "*una bella donna—magnifica,*" or else "*una donna bruta—stupida e schifosa!*" Seated at the head of the table and flanked on either side by a pretty woman (the hostess unselfishly saw to that), Toscanini, his eyes flashing, talked quickly and passionately, his hoarse, raucous, guttural voice holding everyone's attention. This voice, by ordinary standards strident and unlovely, seemed to rise from some deep, seething well of the emotions, and it spoke directly to the senses with the force of strange music. Like music, it outlawed reason. However outrageous the Maestro's opinions might actually be, the emotional urgency of the voice which spoke them made them for the moment utterly convincing and incontrovertible. The colleague, the friend, the foe, the political or civil figure, the musician, painter, writer, or composer the Maestro was pillorying found no defender in that room. Any possible defense could but fall flat

15

after the Maestro's hoarsely ejaculated *"Imbecille! Porco! Ignorante!"*

The Maestro especially bore down heavily on musicians in general and on his colleagues in particular. Most conductors, living or dead, were to him anathema. This one was a "pig" because he re-seated his orchestra on unorthodox lines, bunching the first and second violins, thus upsetting the time-honored arrangement of the two string sections on either side of the conductor, which should resemble, the Maestro maintained, "a pair of shoulders with a head between." That one, an *"assassino"* who dispensed with the baton altogether, disdaining honest up- and down beats, made ridiculous, incomprehensible passes in the air with his hands, to the confusion of orchestra and audience. Also consigned to perdition were the extravagantly out-and-out *physical* conductors, the crouchers, the leapers, the forward-and-backward-bending gymnasts—in fine, the whole tribe of show-offs and charlatans "who think only to themselves, to their frock, to how they look from the back" and "think not at all to the music."

Someone would ask him if he had known many great men in his time. The Maestro would look thoughtful. "Great?" he repeated, shrugging his shoulders and jutting out his lips in disdain. "That is a big word." Then his face suddenly brightened. "Great was Verdi. . . . Yes, Verdi. He was also a good man," he went on. "His music is like his cha*racter*, strong and honest. He was born a *contadino* [peasant]. He remained a *con-*

tadino all his life. Like me," he added. Verdi had been the Maestro's idol.

"I could have known him better . . . but I was in those days very timid. . . . I did not dare to ask to see him. Now I am sorry. Three times in my life I spoke to Verdi. The first time was at La Scala at the rehearsal of *Otello*. I was a conductor then, but I went to play second cello in the orchestra so I could be near him. In one part I played pianissimo as it was written in my music. Verdi said to me: 'No, no, second cello, I cannot hear you. This is a big theater. You must play louder, *naturale*.' He was right, and I said: 'Si, Maestro.' But he was not happy with the *mise en scène*. No! He was never satisfied. You know, after the first performance of his operas he never came to hear them again. But the *première* of *Otello* was tremendous. I was so excited I could not play my cello. When it was finished I ran quickly home. The house was dark, everybody was asleep. I wake-ed my mother. 'Down on your knees to Verdi!' I commanded her. 'Tonight a miracle happen-ed at La Scala.' My poor mother, she was so frightened. I force-ed her to leave the bed and kneel down on the floor. She thought I must be crazy.

"The second time I saw Verdi? Ah, yes. A long time later I myself was conducting *Otello*. At the rehearsal the *tenore* dragg-ed and dragg-ed, he sing slower and slower. I stopp-ed him. 'Why you sing so slow? That is not the way you sang at the first performance when I play cello in the orchestra.' 'Maestro,' he said, 'I sing

Verdi's own tempo.' 'It cannot be,' I said. 'We will go and ask Verdi.' We came to Verdi. The *tenore* sang. I play the piano. Verdi listen and said to the *tenore*: 'No, no, you are too slow . . . you are too slow. You know, Toscanini, singers forget quickly. . . .'" The word "singers" as he uttered it seemed to bring to mind a spate of musical disasters attributable to vocalists he had worked with; for he now abandoned Verdi and launched into a diatribe against all singers, past and present. Seated around the table were several much-admired concert and opera singers, but the Maestro was not to be deterred by anyone's presence. "They are all *cani* [dogs]," he cried, "*tutti* . . . *tutti* . . . every*bawdy* . . . every*bawdy*."

Mercifully, someone attempted to divert the Maestro's wrath by inquiring about the third time he had spoken to Verdi. The stratagem worked. "Ah, yes!" And his savage expression gave way to one of reminiscent tenderness as he related the circumstance of the last time he saw Verdi alive. He was going to conduct Verdi's last work, the choral *Quattro Pezzi Sacri*, and he called on the composer to discuss matters of tempi and interpretation. "He was very kind," the Maestro said, "so kind. I played the pieces on the piano and he said the tempi were correct. I wished to stay longer, but I was too timid. I had not the courage even to ask him for a picture." Here the Maestro's eyes flashed challengingly and he looked at the guests around the table accusingly. "Never —*never* have I asked any*bawdy* for a picture. *Mai* . . .

18

Mai! And I do not like to give my photograph—only imbe*cile* ask for photographs." The guests smiled indulgently at him; for all of them cherished photographs of the Maestro, which he had freely given and charmingly inscribed. Indeed, one Christmas he had sent a gold medal of his head to every member of his orchestra. He had also presented the medal to members of his family and to several favored ladies of his acquaintance. The head, modeled by the sculptor during one of the unsuspecting Maestro's rehearsals, looked savage in the extreme, with the mouth set hard and the eyes, under beetling eyebrows, flashing ecstatic fury or unbridled hatred, or both. It was, in short, a trinket calculated to strike terror in the beholder. But the men of the orchestra, relishing the truth of the artist's representation in metal, received the portrait with gratitude and unselfishly gave it to their wives, who proudly wore it attached to their bracelets. "Yes," the Maestro insisted, "only imbe*cile* ask for photographs." As he spoke, his unheeding eyes rested on a large, elaborately inscribed photograph of himself standing in a silver frame on the sideboard.

There were also supper parties that the Maestro sat through in silence, occasionally sipping his wine, but refusing all food. At those times the conversation around the table was conducted in a low key. One of the bolder spirits there, a very close friend, perhaps, might attempt to draw out the brooding Maestro with some provocative question. The failure of the ruse made the guests even more uncomfortable than before. The self-conscious people around the board hardly touched the food. A second helping in the presence of the abstemious and glowering Maestro was unthinkable. For, notwithstanding a reputation for astigmatism, the Maestro, at certain moments, could see clearly at any distance. He might even launch into a tirade against gourmandizing, beginning with "I cannot understand why people eat so much. I? I do not like to eat. No. For me, sometimes a little soup and bread. This morning at five o'clock I drink a cup of *minestrone* and eat a *grisini* [Italian bread stick]. That is all. I would like to eat *never!*" And he relapsed into silence and looked accusingly at the other guests, some of whom hastily put down their knives and forks, while the anxious hostess made signs to the waiters to clear the table for the *espresso*.

I discovered early that music was the one subject that never failed to dissipate the Maestro's unsocial moods. A disingenuous question on my part like "Do you consider *Falstaff* a masterpiece, Maestro?" would instantly dispel the blackest depression and set him off on a passionate exposition of the glories of that work. "*Falstaff* is a jewel. What a pity you don't know Italian! You must know Italian to understand how wonderfully Verdi fitted together words and music. Do not speak of *Die Meistersinger*. Yes, I know that is also a master*piece*. But not like *Falstaff*. No. *Falstaff* is alone. No Wagner, no German could compose *Falstaff*, only an Italian, only a true Mediterranean like Verdi. *Die Meistersinger* is good, very good, but it is heavy, heavy. *So heavy. Falstaff* is light, it is quick*silver.* You know when I accepted to go to Salzburg I said to Bruno Walter, who was selecting the operas: 'Walter, I wish to conduct *Falstaff.*' He look-ed surprised, because in Salzburg they think to play only Mozart, Beethoven, Wagner, Weber, and Strauss. Why not? I ask-ed him. *Falstaff* is a master*piece,* no? It is a master*piece* like *Fidelio,* like *Magic Flute,* like *Meistersinger.* Oh, yes. If I cannot conduct *Falstaff,* I stay away altogether. No *Falstaff,* no Toscanini."

Another effective gambit was the mention of something that was certain to rouse his ire. "Maestro, last night I went to the Metropolitan . . ." The Maestro did not wait for me to finish. "Don't speak to me of the Metropoli*tan,*" he shouted. "It is a pigsty, not an opera house. They should burn it down. It was a bad theater even forty years ago. Many times I was invited to come to the Metropoli*tan,* but I always said no. Caruso, Scotti, would come to Milan and tell me: 'No, Maestro, the Metropoli*tan* is no theater for you. It is good for make the money, but it is not *serious.*' " I broke in to ask why he finally came to the Metropolitan. "Ah! I came because they tell me one day that Gustav Mahler had accepted to come, and I think to myself if a good moosician like Mahler go there the Metropoli*tan* could not be *too* bad." A pleasant expression suffused his face as he began reliving his seven years (1908–15) at the Metropolitan. We listened to the rich and violent memories of those days. He held us with his vivid descriptions of persons and events. We were aware of the privilege of listening to him, all the more as we were certain that what we heard would never be committed to paper by him. Though his talent for writing, as evidenced by the quality of the letters he wrote, is of a high order, he is as averse to writing about himself as he is to others writing about him. "I am a moosician, not a writer." That simple statement also cut short all requests for interviews and the pressure of agents, photographers, and hero-worshippers.

I learned in time to turn his attention to any musical subject about which I sought enlightenment. He was easily diverted. Notwithstanding his undisciplined nature (undisciplined, that is, outside of music), there was a canny streak in him which often put him wise to the hidden motives of people around him. Yet he could be naïve to a degree. I determined to draw him out on the subject nearest my heart, music, without appearing to be importunate. For my own benefit and that of posterity he must never suspect that he was being pumped.

He had known Richard Strauss intimately. I knew he valued highly the tone poems and *Salome* (unaccountably, he disliked *Der Rosenkavalier*), but I wanted his opinion of the composer's character. From experience I knew that a direct question would not produce the subjective opinion I desired to get from him. "Maestro," I asked, affecting innocence, "is Richard Strauss anything like Verdi? . . . I mean in character, not in music." Instantly he reacted in the expected way

—he gave me a look that was a mixture of scorn and incredulity. "No!" he exploded, "not in *music*, and not in char*acter*." I pretended surprise. He went on in a flood of Italian, but, suddenly remembering that I understood very little of the language, he switched to English without pausing and with no lessening of intensity.

"I will tell you about Strauss. . . . In May, the year 1906, May 25th, yes [the fabulous memory was operating easily], I wrote to him. I ask-ed him for permission to give the first performance of *Salome* in Italy at La Scala. He repli-ed yes. I put the date for the *première* in Milan—December 26. . . . He again repli-ed yes. Very good. But wait, wait," the Maestro said dramatically, "*aspetta . . . aspetta*. . . . One day I read in the newspaper that Strauss himself would give *Salome* in Turin one week *before* my performance in Milan! *Santa*. . . . *Madonna*. . . . *Santissima*. . . . I was a*stone*-ied. I was crazy. I could not eat. . . . I could not sleep. That night I took the train for Vienna, and the next morning I stood before him in his house. 'Strauss,' I told him, 'as a *moosician* I take off my hat to you . . . *aspetta* . . . *aspetta*. . . . But as a *man* . . . I put *on* ten hats!' " and the Maestro, his face shining with scorn, feverishly put on ten imaginary hats.

The graphic dumb show delighted the assembly. Other questions about contemporary musicians were asked, and the Maestro disposed of them as vividly and comprehensively as he had of Strauss. So the night wore on to everyone's satisfaction. The party broke up at a very late hour, the Maestro politely remaining till the last guest had departed. This was a strikingly handsome young lady who had sat at his right the entire evening. He had shown her marked attention, often patting her hand and even urging her to eat, in itself a sign of special interest. The young lady now said good-night to the Maestro and told him how sorry she would be to miss his performance of Beethoven's *Missa Solemnis* with the Philharmonic the following Thursday. She had, she said, long ago accepted an invitation to see *Hot-Cha* that evening. The Maestro pressed her hand understandingly. "Yes, yes," he said, "certainly, certainly," and there was a note of envy in his voice. The Maestro read the advertisements in the papers and knew that *Hot-Cha* was Broadway's biggest musical-comedy hit. He was himself very fond of musical shows. He hoped that some night he, too, would be invited to see *Hot-Cha*.

CHAPTER TWO

$\mathcal{S}$OME time before I met him I had written a short and highly laudatory profile of Toscanini for *The New Yorker*. As the Maestro disapproved of all persons who wrote about him, I was sure he would sooner or later find a way to punish me. Every time I visited him in the green room of Carnegie Hall, I expected the ax to fall. But months went by and nothing happened. When half a year had uneasily passed, I discreetly asked one of his close friends what the Maestro thought of the piece. To my relief and, secretly, to my annoyance, I learned that the Maestro had not seen the article and, when told about it, had not even expressed a desire to read it. The fancied danger thus averted, I approached the Maestro one day after a concert and boldly invited him to dinner at my house. To understand my astonishment at my temerity, imagine a young baseball enthusiast inviting Joe DiMaggio to dinner, or a student of mathematics offering to entertain

Albert Einstein. Indeed, I was so unprepared for an acceptance that when the Maestro replied: "Why not?" I ran all the way home to tell the great news to my family.

My wife, who shared my awe of, and enthusiasm for, Toscanini, flatly refused to believe me. And when I at last convinced her, her delight was tempered by the hazards of the operation: Whom to ask with the Maestro? What to serve? How to behave? These and other questions had to be faced and settled.

We made a list of possible guests. Many turned out to be questionable: one was once divorced; another was addicted to ultramodern music, which the Maestro heartily detested, and so on, and so on. We finally decided to take no risks. We invited three of the Maestro's closest friends—one lady and two gentlemen—who, as far as we knew, had not at the moment incurred his displeasure. As for the menu, my wife sought the advice of the lady. To show our gratitude for the privilege of entertaining the Maestro, my wife extravagantly proposed caviar for an hors d'œuvre, but the lady raised her hands in horror. Caviar belonged to the fish category, and the Maestro never ate fish. Indeed, his feelings about fish were so positive that he had been known to flee from a house where he had merely *sniffed* its presence. Soup, yes. Perhaps a veal *cotoletto*. When in good mood, the Maestro might eat a mouthful or two of *cotoletto*, but very few vegetables. Perhaps a potato. *Espresso*, of course. For drink, champagne and red wine. Later, brandy. He loved to dunk a piece of sugar in brandy, put a match to it, and call everybody's attention to the blue flames in the glass.

That settled, a situation arose at home; learning of the Maestro's impending visit, my parents-in-law, my wife's sister, and a man who was our best and oldest friend flatly insisted on being present. I said no, categorically. My parents-in-law could come in after dinner (should all have gone well by then), but not the other two. The only way, I said jokingly, my sister-in-law and our best friend could be present would be as maid and butler. The two pounced on the idea. Though my wife and I regarded the proposed deception with misgivings, they begged and pleaded and promised to be letter-perfect in the discharge of their duties; and we finally acquiesced. My sister-in-law spent hours carrying trays from the kitchen to the dining-room, and my friend, after many tries, proved to us that he could open the front door with the elegant obsequiousness of a Park Avenue butler (we lived in an unfashionable street on the upper West Side).

An hour before dinner on the fateful day the "maid," clad in an apron and cap, and the "butler" in starched shirt and tails, presented themselves for our inspection. They seemed presentable enough, though my wife thought her sister looked somewhat too presentable. Indeed, except in musical comedies, I had never seen a maid look so fetching. We sat around nervously smoking cigarettes and wishing we had never embarked on an adventure so fraught with peril. At last the doorbell rang, and our hearts practically stopped beating. The butler ran downstairs, ushered the Maestro and his party upstairs into the living-room, and discreetly retired.

I had never seen the Maestro look so forbidding. He greeted us perfunctorily, sat down in an armchair aggressively, and began twirling his mustache. We hovered about, tongue-tied. The butler came in with champagne and the Maestro silently took a glass. Only when the maid appeared with a tray of hors d'œuvres did the atmosphere lighten. The Maestro took out his pince-nez, held it sideways, and with his right eye regarded her through the upper lens. My sister-in-law blushed, and looked outrageously pretty. The Maestro put away his glasses and chose a slice of Italian salami wrapped around a bread stick. He had brightened up remarkably. He began to talk. Conversation became animated. The butler announced dinner and we filed into the dining-room. The soup was brought in. There ensued a tense moment as the Maestro dipped an exploratory spoon in his plate. He raised the spoon to his lips, tasted the soup, smiled, and, like one conferring a degree, said: *"Buono."* The dinner was plain sailing after that. The gentlemen followed the maid with their eyes as she moved around the table. The Maestro took a *cotoletto* and gave her an approving look as he helped himself. The guests told anecdotes, mainly about the Maestro, who listened approvingly and supplied accurate names and dates, and sometimes took over and elaborated a story that someone had just begun. The dinner over, we rose and went into the living-room. The brandy was served, the piece of sugar was lighted, and the glass was filled with blue flame, to the Maestro's satisfaction and everybody's delight. The maid came into the room very frequently to empty ash trays and tidy up. This annoyed my wife, who attempted by surreptitious signs to induce her sister not to come in again. But the latter, flushed with success, remorselessly came and went until the party took their leave. When the front door closed on them, the butler ran up the stairs two at a time laughing and fell exhausted on a living-room sofa. The maid lit a cigarette and danced around the room in triumph. The party had been a success; the deception had come off perfectly. We relived every moment of the evening. But in the midst of our rejoicing someone remarked: "What if he finds out?"

That dinner was the beginning of a close friendship. The Maestro thereafter came often to our house, but familiarity failed to dull the wonder and delight we felt in his company. We learned by trial and error how best to amuse him; we discovered, for example, a naïveté we had not suspected. Like most Italians, he was short on humor, but he adored slapstick, practical jokes, and all manner of juvenile games, especially those which involved deceptions. One night when the company rose from the dinner table, we noticed that the fringed silk gown of one of the ladies had been mysteriously chewed away up to her knees. After a moment of bewilderment, we traced the crime to our young mischievous cocker spaniel, who had crept under the table and silently nibbled at the dress. The Maestro, on learning this, grew purple with laughter at the lady's discomfiture, and even pleaded for clemency for the dog.

Somewhere on Sixth Avenue there is, or there used to be, a delightful shop called The House of Fun, where one could purchase trick objects and contraptions designed to fool unsuspecting guests at parties. With these we fooled the Maestro many times, always to his own delight. One object consisted of several pieces of metal loosely tied together. The maid dropped the pieces on the kitchen floor, with a noise like that of many dishes breaking. My wife pretended that she had heard nothing and went on talking to the Maestro, whose sensitive ears had reacted violently to the sound. Five minutes later the metal was again dropped, and again my wife disregarded the clamor. But this time the Maestro could not contain himself. "Pauline," he demanded, "go to the kitchen! Some *stupido* is breaking all your dishes!" He had an uncomfortable experience with a brandy glass that had a tiny hole in it. Each time he raised it to his lips a few drops of the liquor spilled on his shirt front. A most fastidious man, the Maestro could not comprehend what was happening, and furtively wiped the drops with his handkerchief. When we could stand his discomfiture no longer, we revealed the trick, and his relief was immense. But he was impatient to try it himself on some unsuspecting friend.

One day we took him into our confidence and asked him to join us in tricking his wife. The Maestro enthusiastically agreed, and we showed him our latest purchase from The House of Fun, an ordinary table knife that broke in half when applied to the cutting of meat. This knife was placed next to a bona-fide fork beside Mrs. Toscanini's dinner plate. The Maestro could hardly wait for dinner to be announced. He sat opposite his wife at table and watched her narrowly when the meat course came around. To his consternation (and ours), the cook had baked a meat loaf and Mrs. Toscanini used only her fork. There ensued an exchange of words in Italian between husband and wife. The Maestro said sharply: "Carla! Have you no knife?" To which his wife replied that she had a knife, but the meat was soft and did not require one. The Maestro grew angry. "What nonsense! One does not eat meat without a knife! Where are your manners? Where were you brought up?" She looked up in astonishment. "What is the matter with you, Papá? I don't need a knife." *"Per Dio Santo,"* the Maestro cried in desperation, "you do, you do! Use your knife, like a civilized person! Like me! Like every*bawdy* here. . . . So!" and he ostentatiously cut into his meat. Completely mystified, she shrugged her shoulders, but to avoid a scene, she took up the knife and used it. The knife did what was expected of it, and the Maestro, who had watched its application apprehensively, laughed with glee; and his wife, who herself was not above enjoying a practical joke, joined in. That winter we drew heavily on The House of Fun. It is true that our plans for gay dinner parties often went awry, for everything depended on the

Maestro's disposition during the day, the evening, and up to the dinner hour. But our successes outnumbered our failures. One time we were horrified to learn that one of the guests who had been present at our very first dinner party had in a moment of weakness revealed to the Maestro the trick we had played on him with a false maid and butler. But to our great relief the Maestro, far from resenting it, regarded it as a capital joke, and went around telling it to his friends with vivid gestures and in minute detail. Emboldened by this success, we staged a similar deception. This time my sister-in-law was again disguised as a maid, but an ill-dressed, disheveled, slovenly one, with blackened teeth. When she served the Maestro he could not conceal his aversion, and he refused all food to avoid getting close to her. At the end of dinner, the "waitress" deposited her tray of ice cream on the table and, without warning, seated herself on the Maestro's lap, threw her arms around him, and planted a kiss on his cheek. The Maestro's frozen look of horror defies all description. But the next moment the maid revealed her identity, and his anguished look gave place to one of incredulity and pleasure.

Another evening, he bounded up the stairs to our living-room and was met by a strange sight: our family, all arrayed in eighteenth-century costumes and headgear, stood at the top of the staircase ready to greet him with appropriate period elegance. This was so unexpected that he became utterly confused. "You said not to dress," he murmured, as he began running down the stairs to the street door. Only when he was brought back and got a closer look did he realize that we were outfitted in the formal evening attire of two hundred years back.

These bizarre incidents he never tired of relating. His favorite story concerned one that occurred in our house, but for once without our foreknowledge. We had invited the Maestro and his wife to dinner. At the last moment two of the other guests telephoned their regrets. As we were chatting in the living-room after dinner, there was a violent ringing of the doorbell, and presently our maid hurried into the room. There was a taxicab in front of the house, she said; in it was a horse, and the horse had demanded a dollar and a quarter to pay for the cab. I ran downstairs and into the street, and there indeed stood a cab with the front and rear of a horse protruding out the windows. The front said hoarsely: "For God's sake, pay the driver and let us out of here!" I recognized the voice as that of one of our absent friends. I paid the driver and opened the door; the horse sprang out, bounded up the stairs and into the living-room, which it circled innumerable times, circus fashion, and at last collapsed on the floor in a heap.

All this time the Maestro, who got to his feet in amazement when the horse stampeded into the room, followed its gyrations with eyes starting from his head. (His version of the incident, which he repeated for years at every opportunity, grew in dramatic intensity with each telling, accompanied by flashing eyes and intensive gestures, and was frequently punctuated with the inquiry

"*È vero?*" addressed to Mrs. Toscanini, who always listened to the tale excitedly, and always answered solemnly: "*Sì! È vero!*") When the two human components of the horse extricated themselves, they revealed the details of the hoax, which was indeed an elaborate affair requiring secrecy, much persuasion (to get a cabdriver to bring them), and serious practice in equine behavior, especially by the one who was the rear of the horse. But the pair agreed that the reaction of the Maestro as he pointed to the crazily circling horse and shouted: "*Guarda,* Carla! *Cavallo! Cavallo!*" was a sufficient reward for all their pains.

The relish with which Toscanini entered into such innocent pastimes seemed to be in inverse ratio to the ever-present spiritual agonies of his musical life. They offered surcease from the grave soul-searchings that musical scores and their translation into sound imposed on him, and from the great bouts with his orchestra, and his desperate attempts to make it a flawless medium for his own reconstruction of the printed page. The Toscanini who watched the progress of some practical joke with impish expectancy and uninhibited joy was quite different from the one who stayed up half the night wrestling with the scores of the great masters of music, who each morning locked himself in rehearsal combat with his orchestra. For the Toscanini rehearsals were, in the main, deadly battles between conductor and orchestra, and even between Toscanini and himself. And one of the reasons his players did not rebel against the insult and injury he heaped on them was the tongue-lashings the Maestro inflicted on himself when he found he could not communicate his own vision to his men. At those times he castigated himself as an incompetent man, a bad musician, a conductor unworthy to command an orchestra. "It is not your fault," he would say. "No! Not at all. It is mine. I am the *stupido*. I cannot make this pig of an arm" (and he hacked furiously at his right arm with his left) "say what I wish . . . what the composer wants. . . ." And, awed by the agony mirrored in his expressive face, the men pitied him and forgot their own troubles. He could hurt their self-esteem, but they fought against resentment, for they saw plainly that their tormentor suffered, too, as only a man defeated in realizing an ideal of perfection can suffer. After a grueling session with an orchestra he could passionately say to me: "I feel they [the players] are my enemy. I want to *kill* them. It would give me pleasure . . . they are against me . . . they are beasts . . . yes, beasts." His look at that moment was demonic. And just as Benvenuto Cellini (whom the Maestro resembled in artistic rectitude, courage, recklessness, and vindictiveness) harbored—and often translated into action—thoughts of murder against real or fancied enemies, so Toscanini, four hundred years later, often brooded on revenge and bemoaned the effete times that stood in the way of his taking simple, direct action. For him there was something wrong with an age that frowned on dire punishment for miscreants who defiled the sacred art of music.

If he could not actually slay an "opponent," he could at least be brutally pitiless in his abuse. The Marquis de Sade himself would have been hard put to invent anything like the verbal tortures Toscanini visited on some unfortunate player. He staged harrowing inquisitions, which he built up with the deliberation of a crafty playwright. At a rehearsal one day a member of the orchestra had just got through a solo passage, when the Maestro rapped for silence. He assumed a pose, hand on hip and baton touching the end of his nose gingerly, which the men knew from long experience signified displeasure and the framing of a suitable punishment. An ominous silence pervaded the room as the Maestro stood meditatively tapping the end of his nose. Then, suddenly, he brightened up and called the player by name. The man said eagerly: "Yes, Maestro," and rose to his feet. The Maestro contemplated him benevolently for a few moments. Then he said pleasantly: "Tell me, please, when were you born?" The man, wondering, told him. "And in what month?" the Maestro pursued evenly. The man stammered out the month. "And what day?" The man, now completely unnerved, had to think, and the Maestro waited, patiently tapping his nose. At length the man said weakly: "I think it was a Tuesday, Maestro." Then the Maestro pounced. *"That,"* he shouted at the startled musician, "was a black day for music!" He raised his baton in the air and poised it for a downbeat. "And now, *da capo!* [from the beginning]" he commanded. The dreadful moment for the solo passage arrived and passed. This time it was quite another story. The Maestro, still beating away, was heard above the fortissimo sound of the orchestra: "So! So!" and with his left hand threw a kiss to the so recently crucified player. "Like this! Like this! So you are *not* stupid. You *can* play well. . . . Santa Madonna . . . Santissima . . . Now *I* am happy. . . . *You* are happy. . . . *Beethoven* is happy. . . ." At the final chord of the movement the Maestro put down his baton and turned smilingly to the concertmaster. "You know," he began, and the orchestra to a man leaned forward to catch every word, "I remember me a moosician in La Scala, it must be forty years ago . . . yes, in 1906 . . . the month was February . . . yes . . . February the fourteenth, a Saturday . . . I was conducting *Tosca* . . . his name was Bertelli . . . Giovanni Bertelli . . . he was a wonderful player . . . but *stupido* . . . no, not *stupido* . . . *stu-pi-dis-simo!*" The men listened eagerly to the anecdote, laughing loudly and nervously at the humorous moments and exchanging meaningful glances at each evidence of the Maestro's prodigious memory. Forgotten was the vitriolic little dialogue the Maestro had so cleverly staged a moment before. Dispelled was the orchestra's uneasiness. Even the unfortunate player was now forgiving and happy.

There were times when the Maestro shed the four centuries that separated him from the Italian Renaissance in an instant and behaved as uninhibitedly as Benvenuto Cellini. Once, in his younger days at La

Scala, he impulsively threw his baton at the head of an erring violinist, catching him painfully in the eye. The man sued for physical damages and the hurt to his self-esteem. The trial was a stirring spectacle, with all Milan divided on the merits of the case. Toscanini put up a spirited defense, contending that his assault was strictly impersonal, merely the reflex action of a sensitive artist in defense of his art. In the end he was morally exonerated, but he had to pay several thousand lire toward the violinist's medical expenses. It was a considerable sum for those days, but the Maestro paid cheerfully, deeming it not excessive in return for the satisfaction he felt in defending his art.

Many years later he again succumbed to a sixteenth-century impulse. A difference had arisen between two members of the NBC Symphony Orchestra. The Maestro heard about it and generously offered to interview the two and resolve the quarrel. He summoned the men to his dressing-room and asked each to state his grievance. He heard the first one out patiently, then politely turned to the second, who launched into his grievance glibly and confidently. As he proceeded, the Maestro's face darkened. Before the man could finish, the Maestro, trembling with emotion, roared: "Stop! You are not saying the truth . . . you are not a *man* . . . you speak lies!" And with clenched fists he began to beat him about the head. Taken unawares by this sudden transformation, the player stood dazed and rooted to the spot, suffering the blows to rain on his head. Then, recovering,

38

he fled from the room, toward the elevators and safety, the Maestro in hot pursuit. But before the old man (Toscanini was then seventy-five years old) could catch up with him, an NBC official threw himself on the volcanic Maestro, pinned his arms behind him, and led him, wildly protesting, back to his dressing-room. There the Maestro, pale and exhausted, threw himself on a couch, clutched at his head, and for a quarter of an hour breathed stertorously, like one about to give up the ghost.

Yet the injured and aggrieved player harbored no malice. Prudently, for a time he kept at a distance from the orchestra and its Maestro. But some months later he wrote his assailant, politely requesting an interview. This the Maestro granted. He received his visitor at his Riverdale home, chatted amiably, listened sympathetically, and rang for *espresso*. Indeed, the Maestro behaved so charmingly that there could be little doubt that he had quite forgotten the intensity of his reaction to his original meeting with the player in his dressing-room at NBC. As for the visitor, it seemed never to have occurred to him to bring charges against the Maestro at Local 802, the New York branch of the American Federation of Musicians. Local 802 is a tough organization, pledged to uphold the dignity of its members. A harsh word to a member is an insult to the Union, and no complaint of mistreatment is too insignificant to result in immediate inquiry and appropriate action. Once, at a rehearsal with the NBC Symphony, a celebrated guest conductor reprimanded a violinist for inattention. The rebuke was mild enough. But a half-hour later a delegate from 802 appeared and brusquely told the conductor to apologize to the violinist in the presence of the orchestra then and there, or be yanked from the podium. The conductor, somewhat nonplused, acquiesced. But no charges of any kind were ever lodged against Toscanini. The plain truth is that all his life he has been forgiven conduct that would have been tolerated in no other artist. With no outside force to back him up, he was in his own realm an absolute dictator. For one thing, his glamorous hold on the public made victory in any open contest with a disaffected player, singer, agent, or impresario a foregone conclusion. For another, there was the undeniable fact of his unique stature as a musician, his fearlessness as a man, the beguiling charm of his personality, the startling vividness of the figure as a whole. It seemed to be universally agreed that he was not subject to the rules and regulations that applied to other men, even to other celebrated artists.

When the effects of his encounters at morning rehearsals wore off sufficiently during the day for him to be in a mood to come to dinner, we felt more than ever obliged to devise some entertainment that would erase from his memory his earlier session with his orchestra. On one such evening we introduced him to the "murder" game. This consisted in dealing out playing-cards to the participants. The holder of the ace of spades was the would-be "murderer," a fact known to that person alone. The lights went out and players milled around in the dark room, trying to ward off the "murderer." When the "murderer" placed his hands on his "victim," that person would count ten to give the "assassin" time to lose himself in the crowd, then let out a piercing scream and fall to the floor. The lights came on, everyone stood frozen, and the district attorney (previously selected) questioned each player. Only the murderer was permitted to lie; everyone else had to speak the truth.

When the "murder" game was outlined to him, the Maestro showed interest, but declined to be an active participant. Before the lights went out he took up an inconspicuous position between the piano and the wall, as the safest place for a spectator. There followed a few minutes of darkness; a scream duly rent the air; the lights came on. The Maestro had not moved an inch. His face, however, was mysteriously covered with lipstick. The "district attorney" asked him whether anyone had approached him during the blackout. "No!" the Maestro answered simply, "no-bawdy." He came from behind the piano. He listened with grave attention to the "trial" and the "evidence" and marveled at the "district attorney's" success in exposing the murderer. He confessed he like-ed the game, and thereafter always welcomed the suggestion to play it.

The Maestro was enthusiastic about the theater, more especially about musical comedy. During his years at the Metropolitan (1908–15) he saw many Broadway musicals. His favorite was *The Pink Lady*, whose waltz number ("Beautiful Lady") he admired and sometimes played on the piano when in reminiscent mood. Feeling sure that he would welcome an evening at a musical play, I made up a party to dine and to go on to see Ethel Merman in her musical hit *Panama Hattie*. And, indeed, the prospect of an evening at the theater pleased him and he arrived for dinner in the gayest of moods. Sitting opposite him at the table were my nine-year-old daughter Anne and my twelve-year-old son Blair, who had been permitted to come downstairs so that they might carry through life the memory of having dined with Toscanini. Throughout dinner, Anne never took her eyes off the Maestro; Blair, however, was unimpressed. He soon began to exhibit symptoms of ennui; and at one point, in the middle of an anecdote of the Maestro's childhood days at Parma, Blair took from his pocket two little magnets. He laid one of them on the table in front of him and held the other a few inches over it. The two magnets promptly sprang together, whereupon Blair separated them and repeated his game.

The Maestro, still talking, focused his gaze on the magnets. Presently his words trailed off into an incoherent murmur. He was giving his entire attention to Blair. "That's a magnet, Maestro," I said. "Yes," he said, "a *magneto*. I know." "Would you like them?" He nodded eagerly. "Blair, give the magnets to the Maestro." Blair made no move to obey. "Come on, Blair, hand them over," I commanded. But Blair had put the magnets back into his pocket. "Gee, Dad, I can't," he said, "it don't belong to me. It's my friend Sam's." I spoke more sternly to Blair, who kept doggedly denying his ownership and insisting that he could not possibly do as he was told. The Maestro followed this interchange keenly, his eyes veering from me to my son and back again as if his fate depended on the outcome. The situation grew painful. Blair was plainly determined not to give up the magnets. Concealing as best I could my chagrin at my son's behavior, I finally broke down Blair's resistance with hints of enough money to buy a dozen *magnetos*. The magnets were grudgingly handed over. The Maestro pocketed them with satisfaction and resumed his interrupted anecdote.

It was a charming story of his early home life in Parma, where he was born. The Toscaninis, he said, were very poor. The little Arturo (he was an only son) went hungry, the family diet (when it materialized) consisted mainly of bread and soup. "That is why I like soup and bread all my life," he beamed. "I am a peasant, like Verdi. One day my doctor said to me: 'Toscanini, you are well-born.' He means I was born a peasant, strong and simple! My mother was strong, very strong, in body and in char*acter*. My father no! He was very handsome. In my house in Milano I have a beautiful picture of him in a Garibaldi shirt and a Vandyke beard. He was a good man, but weak. He like-ed to drink." (The Maestro graphically shoved his thumb into his mouth and tilted his head back, by way of illustration.) "He was a tailor —in those days, you know, I wish-ed to be a tailor, too,

I would take scissors and cut cloth. The shop was in our living-room. Sometimes the neighbors came and brought their sewing, these people they like-ed to work together in Parma. While they work-ed some*bawdy* read aloud from a book. In this way I learn-ed many, many books. *Ee-van-o-eh, I Miserabili, Il Gobbo di Notre Dame, I Promessi Sposi*, Dante, Shakespeare. I lov-ed these books. And music, too, I learn-ed when I was a little child. Oh yes, in Parma every*bawdy* like-ed music. The people were critical in Parma—more than in Rome, more than in Milano. You know, singers were afraid to come to Parma. The same *tenore* who made a success at La Scala could make a terrible fiasco in Parma." (The Maestro shoved the second and fourth fingers of his right hand into his mouth as if to whistle, to indicate the Parmesan reaction to some vainglorious vocalist.)

According to Toscanini, everybody in his native town knew the standard operas. In the Toscanini workshop–living-room the workers frequently broke into song and little Arturo knew the arias and ensemble numbers of many operas long before he learned to read music or saw the inside of an opera house. Music, so learned at secondhand, was sometimes likely to be inaccurate. Of this Arturo, of course, was blissfully unaware. So much so, that when he was taken to the gallery of the Parma Opera House to hear his first opera, Verdi's *Un Ballo in Maschera*, he was shocked to hear the tenor sing a certain aria in a manner that he, the child Toscanini, considered wrong. "No, no! You are wrong!" the little boy in the gallery, cupping his hands, shouted at the astonished tenor on the stage. "It goes like this . . ." and the child sang out the tune with all the imperfections he had learned at home.

While he was telling us of his early privations and enthusiasms, the Maestro frequently put his hand into the pocket of his jacket to make sure that the *magnetos* were still there. We left our house early and got to the theater while it was fairly empty ("Artists should never be kept waiting"). The Maestro awaited the rise of the curtain with the eagerness of a child. He laughed extravagantly at Miss Merman's down-to-earth deportment and admired her lung power. In the first intermission he stood up and swept the audience with his opera glasses, quite unaware that the people had caught sight of him and were all looking at him. A man came up and said: "Excuse me, are you Maestro Toscanini?" The Maestro, not turning a hair, answered innocently: "No. I am sorry," and the man, incredulous and still gazing at him, retreated.

Near the end of the play I saw that the Maestro was not paying attention to the stage. I whispered: "Is anything wrong?" and he whispered back: "The *magnetos*. I have lost them!" I told him not to worry, that he must have dropped them on the floor, and when the curtain came down we would look for them. Until the end of the play he sat, the picture of dejection, his right hand propping up his head, his eyes closed. When the curtain descended, we waited ten minutes for the theater to empty. We then got down on our hands and knees and searched for the *magnetos*. We called over the ushers and they searched the lobbies, but all to no avail. We left the theater and got into the Maestro's car. Usually, after theater, we drove to our house, where we discussed the play, drank brandy, and the Maestro talked and played the piano until early in the morning. This time the Maestro said he preferred to go home. When the car stopped at our house I suggested that he might have dropped the *magnetos* on our doorstep on the way to the theater. "You think?" the Maestro said, brightening, and he jumped nimbly out of the car and, along with the rest of us, began searching our stoop, illuminated by a street lamp. There the *magnetos* lay in full view. I picked them up and gave them to the Maestro, who hastily put them in his pocket and suddenly decided he was "thirty" (thirsty) and wanted to drink "some*thing*." Mrs. Toscanini demurred, saying it was late and that her husband had a concert the following afternoon. The Maestro packed her off to their hotel. As the car drove away he commented: "Poor Carla! She is always sleeping. She is old." (She was ten years his junior.) We went upstairs, where he drank some*thing*, talked for hours, to our delight, played the piano and sang large chunks of operas in his cracked voice. It was six in the morning before he left reluctantly. The sun had risen and birds were twittering. "I could conduct a concert this moment," he said as he loudly sniffed the morning air. We had no doubt that he could. There was a chill in the air, but he disdained to put on his overcoat. He regarded me pity-ingly as I shivered on the doorstep and magnanimously advised me to go inside before I caught cold. When he reached his hotel suite (he told me subsequently) he removed his shoes like any conscience-stricken husband who had been out late and feared to disturb his wife. An hour later the maid brought him his morning coffee. He spent the morning in study. The afternoon concert went off without incident and to his satisfaction. In the green room later, I asked him if he felt fatigued after staying up all night. "No!" he said. "When I enjoy what I do, I am never tired. Nothing that I like to do can be bad for me."

CHAPTER THREE

$\mathcal{I}$N the summer of 1930 Toscanini was invited by Siegfried Wagner, son of the great Richard, to conduct
Tannhäuser and *Tristan* at the Bayreuth Festival in
Bavaria. This was a revolutionary step. No Italian conductor had ever been remotely considered for the sacred
German festival; but Toscanini's fame and drawing-
power had penetrated even there. He was asked to name
a fee, but refused, saying that he considered the honor
of conducting at Bayreuth sufficient payment. I was
planning to be in Europe that summer and was eager
to go to Bayreuth. The Maestro asked me to call on him
there.

This was the year of the real emergence of Nazism
in Germany, and especially in Bavaria. Adolf Hitler was
an ardent Wagnerite, and he and some of his lieutenants
were to attend the Festival. His presence was expected to
stimulate the box office, but it was Toscanini who proved

to be the real star of the season, which had been quickly sold out on the announcement of his coming.

Bayreuth was so crowded that summer that it was with great difficulty that I found a place to sleep. It was my first visit; I had expected to find a lovely town, an ideal setting for a Wagner shrine. In reality Bayreuth was an ugly, smoky little community, its architecture hideous and its inhabitants ungracious and even rude. On the afternoon of the performance of *Tannhäuser* I joined the German and foreign worshippers (at fifteen dollars a head) who walked the mile or so from the town to the Festspielhaus, an unprepossessing wooden theater perched on the top of a hill. From its roof, trumpeters blaringly warned the faithful that the opera was about to begin. The inside of the theater, though an acoustical marvel, was a perfect firetrap; it was enormously wide, with only two aisles along the far sides. Because there was no middle aisle, the people in each row had to stand until the last person had taken his seat. But once the lights went out and the overture sounded from a completely hidden orchestra pit, the magic of Toscanini filled the theater, and I was treated to a performance of *Tannhäuser* so beautiful and alive that it dwarfed any other presentation I had ever seen.

In the intermission I made my way to the green room, but was stopped by a uniformed official, who put me at the end of a long line of people waiting to see the Maestro. Directly in front of me stood an enormous man in a long green robe, and a distinguished-looking middle-aged woman. The official came around with pad and pencil to take our names. To my surprise, the large man said "Ferdinand—of Bulgaria," and the middle-aged lady, "Princess Margherita" (a relative of Victor Emmanuel, King of Italy). The official disappeared and after a few minutes returned. "The Maestro," he announced in German in a loud voice, "will see Mr. Chotzinoff and Mr. Lodi." Mr. Lodi, a drab little Italian, and I stepped out of line and were conducted to the Maestro's dressing-room.

There sat the Maestro, naked from the waist up, his face in an agony of pain. He was subject to attacks of bursitis, and this one looked unusually severe. A heat lamp was focused on his right shoulder. Near him hovered the German conductor Wilhelm Furtwängler. "*Povero* Toscanini!" the Maestro said, trying to smile. "The shoulder is terrible! When I conduct I forget a little. But this moment the pain is terrible. Terrible!" Nevertheless, he greeted me and Signor Lodi warmly, especially Lodi. "*Come sta, caro* [how are you, my dear]?" he inquired. The Italian beamed and bent down to kiss the Maestro's hand. "Lodi was *cameriere* in the Milano hotel, you know, where Verdi died," the Maestro explained. "A fine *cameriere*, and a good man. . . . *Caro* Lodi . . . I thank you for coming to see an old friend." The two conversed in Italian for a few minutes, and the radiant Lodi took his leave. The Maestro then asked me for news of America, and in turn told me about some of the drawbacks he had encountered in Bayreuth. The most irksome was the obligation of the artists to repair after a performance to the great restaurant adjacent to the opera house, there to be inspected at close range by the audience.

"Of course I refuse-ed," he said indignantly. "I told Winifred [Mrs. Siegfried Wagner] I was not an animal for exhibition in a cage. She begged and cri-ed, and said the people are us-ed to see the artists and conductors after the opera. You know, many people come to Bayreuth just to see. Can you believe? I am ashamed for me, for Wagner. But she beg! Ah! *Caro* Chotzie, the life of a serious moosician is *difficile*. . . . Yet I like very much this theater. This theater is serious. Wagner did well when he made an apron to conceal the conductor and orchestra. N*obawdy* can see them. You know, I must laugh. Furtwängler"—Furtwängler had vanished like a ghost—"likes it not, because n*obawdy* can see him conduct. They tell me he would like to raise the platform for the orchestra and take away the apron so that the audience can see him. . . . *Pensa!* [Imagine!]"

The intermission was about over, and I said good-by. I felt sorry for the people who could not get in to see the Maestro. It occurred to me that perhaps the Maestro had not been told about the King and the Princess. "Did they tell you, Maestro," I asked as I was leaving, "that the King of Bulgaria and the Princess . . ." The Maestro cut me short with a disdainful wave of his arms which doubled him up in pain. "Yes, yes," he shouted, "they told me. But what have I to do with kings and princesses? They have no-*thing* to say to me. I have no-*thing* to say to them. No! I am not happy to see them. I am only happy to see my friends."

A few years later, at a supper party after a "good" concert with the Philharmonic, Toscanini, in an expansive mood, invited my wife and me to visit him the following June at the "Isolino," the little Borromean island on the lake of Maggiore he had rented for a term of years. After a fortnight on the Isolino we would all go to Venice to stay with Toscanini's son-in-law and daughter, the Count and Countess Castelbarco. The Maestro, however, would spend only one night in Venice and then fly to Salzburg, where he was to conduct several operas for the Festival. We were to join him there a week later.

In June we sailed for Genoa and from there took a train to Milan. Mrs. Toscanini met us at the station, and we drove on to Pallanza, the town adjacent to the Isolino. It had begun to rain, and by the time we reached Pallanza the rain had become a downpour. We got into a small covered launch and made for the Isolino. As we approached, we discerned a small figure standing at the water's edge; it was the Maestro waiting to receive us. He stood drenched, hatless and coatless, oblivious of the furious rain beating down on him. "At last!" he said solemnly, as he embraced us. "I thought I would never see you again." Servants came running with umbrellas and we climbed the steep hill to the house, the Maestro running nimbly ahead.

It was a beautiful island, full of rare trees and shrubs and exotic flowers. To us it seemed an enchanted isle, the ultimate setting for its magical deity. Toscanini himself showed us through the villa that crowned the island—a redone eleventh-century monastery. Nothing more romantic could be imagined. The terrace and the main rooms and bedrooms opened a hundred feet above Lago Maggiore, its surface now blistered with sharp pebbles of rain. The Maestro enjoyed our delight and promised us greater wonders when the rain would cease and the sun come out. I went to bed that night in a state of unreality, and I could barely close my eyes. Early in the morning, quicksilver fragments of light seeped through the chinks in the shutters. I got out of bed, threw them open, and flooded the room with blinding sunlight. The lake below was a motionless expanse pinpricked by millions of sunbeams. I put on a dressing-gown and went downstairs, stepping softly so as not to be heard. Passing near the kitchen, I heard the Maestro's voice. I went in. The Maestro, in blue silk pajamas, was talking to the cook. I greeted him and asked him why he was up so early. "I came," he said cheerfully, "to order for you an American breakfast—ham and eggs." We then went into the living-room, where he unbolted and threw open all the shutters, arranged chairs, and pottered around busily like a practical servantless householder doing the morning chores. This done, we went outdoors, smelled and admired the flowers, and greeted an aged gardener, with whom the Maestro held an animated conversation. Then we went back and had our breakfast on the terrace, I my ham and eggs, he a cup of soup and bread. He was the soul of solicitude, much concerned that the ham should be to my taste (which it wasn't, though I said it was perfect) and the eggs properly "cook-ed."

After breakfast the Maestro excused himself and went upstairs. He came down again toward noon, dressed smartly in striped trousers, pleated starched shirt, cuffs and collar, and black bow tie. We sat in chairs on the terrace facing the lake. The Maestro's presence on the Isolino drew many sightseers in rowboats and on the ancient paddle boats that made the circuit of the lake. The boats came very close to the Isolino, and people stood up, waved handkerchiefs, and yelled: *"Bravo,* Toscanini! *Viva* Toscanini!" I was touched by this show of affection, but the Maestro's face suddenly darkened and he shouted back: *"Stupido. . . . Ignoranti. . . . Schifoso!"* However, when a small launch came along and those in it did not speak but waved their handkerchiefs or their arms at us, the Maestro smiled and waved back as if he believed they were waving at two anonymous figures.

The week we spent on the Isolino had a fairytale quality. We were taken to visit the other Borromean islands. We steamed over to the Isola dei Pescatori, a quaint, unspoiled fishing-village, and lunched with the

Maestro's great friend Ugo Ara. Ara was once the violist of the celebrated Flonzaley Quartet. When he left the Quartet he went to live on the Isola dei Pescatori. Born a Jew, he had become a convert to Catholicism and given himself up to good works with a zeal and simplicity that endeared him to the fishing-folk and earned him the name of saint. Toscanini took me to Ara's little house, which consisted of a tiny room with only a cot, a small table, and two chairs. The Maestro called my attention to the austerity of Ara's life, and said: "That is the way we should all live." He said it with emotion; he believed what he was saying. But in America, after a visit to Jascha Heifetz's spacious, comfortable, remodeled farmhouse in Connecticut, he told me that such simple surroundings did not suit an artist of Jascha's fame. And neither his own house on the Isolino nor his apartment in Milan approximated the modest dimensions of Ugo Ara's monastic cell.

The Maestro was preparing for his Salzburg season. His music room was piled high with many editions of the score of *Die Meistersinger* and books in all languages relating to Wagner. He had long been familiar with the prose works of Wagner. But now he went laboriously through all the composer's articles and letters for whatever light they might shed on the interpretation, the scenic designs, and the staging of *Die Meistersinger*. At Bayreuth he had discovered a mistake in the orchestral parts of *Tristan*. Since the death of Wagner this error had gone unnoticed. Now he showed me passages in the writings of Wagner which contradicted the traditional staging of the final scene of *Die Meistersinger*. All this was fascinating for me, especially his running comments on Wagner and his music, and his animadversions on the plain disregard of Wagner's wishes by conductors, directors, and singers the world over. The Wagner recitative, which vocalists treated with the freedom permissible only in cadenzas, was meant, he claimed, to be sung in strict time, and he pointed to Wagner's own words to prove it. Though the cast for *Die Meistersinger* in Salzburg would boast seasoned artists, he feared they would be tradition-ridden. They must therefore relearn the opera as if it were a brand-new work. "And what a work it is!" he exclaimed ecstatically. "*Ma . . .*" and he smiled indulgently, "*sempre* C Major [always C Major]. . . . Beautiful, yes . . . but too much C Major."

Suddenly the week was over—like a moment. We left the Isolino and motored to Venice in the Toscanini Cadillac, driven by Emilio, the Maestro's massive Swiss chauffeur and bodyguard. Emilio made the most of his employer's fame. When we stopped for lunch in Verona, he and his car became the center of attention for the passers-by. Surrounded by an eager crowd, Emilio was pleased to answer questions flung at him, no doubt inventing details of the Maestro's habits and idiosyncrasies, though an unvarnished report would in all probability have been even more startling. Actually the drive to Venice was a mixed pleasure for my wife and me. The Maestro had (and still has) a mania for speed, and regarded a seventy-mile-an-hour clip as a leisurely pace. Our expressions of alarm only delighted him. "But we are going *adagio*," he would say disingenuously. "Emilio, a little faster!" And Emilio, who relished his master's pranks, would accelerate the speed of the car to its limit, the unceasing sound of the horn scattering bicycles to the right and left like astonished and resentful chickens.

The Maestro spent only one night in Venice. Early the next morning he flew alone to Salzburg. He carried a valise containing his immediate needs, and his wife tied some money in his handkerchief in the event of an emergency. He departed happily, for he loved traveling, particularly in airplanes. His journey proved safe and uneventful. Some hours later a telegram to that effect arrived from Salzburg.

A week later Mrs. Toscanini, my wife, and I motored to Salzburg. We arrived there toward nightfall and went to the Österreichischer Hof, where the Maestro had stayed the week. Mrs. Toscanini told us to wait in the lobby while she went up to fetch her husband. We would then have dinner in the dining-room. She returned presently, followed by the Maestro. We could read on both their faces that something was amiss. The Maestro looked straight at us with no sign of recognition. We went into the dining-room and sat at a table. A waiter who spoke Italian took Mrs. Toscanini's orders. The Maestro never uttered a word, and hardly touched his food. Nor, for that matter, did my wife and I; we were completely floored by the Maestro's conduct. Din-

ner over, we bade Mrs. Toscanini good-night and went
to our room, where we sat around unhappily trying to
figure out what to do in the strange role of unwanted
guests. We finally decided to remain in Salzburg on our
own, and to avoid meeting the Toscaninis at all costs.

The next morning we went to the Maestro's rehearsal. Afterward, for fear of running into him at the
hotel, we lunched in a restaurant on the edge of the
town. In the evening there was another rehearsal, which
we attended, for we had no intention of letting our personal pique interfere with our enjoyment of the Maestro's art. As we were walking back to the hotel, his car
drew up alongside us and Mrs. Toscanini motioned us
to get in. The Maestro was sitting up front with Emilio,
his usual perch. He now turned on us in a fury. "Where
have you been all this time?" he demanded. "Why did
not you come to dinner tonight?" This seemed even
more incomprehensible than his obliviousness of our
presence the night before. "Well, Maestro," I began
boldly, when I was able to collect my faculties, "after the
way you treated us last night—" "I knew it, I knew it,"
he broke in triumphantly. "You are people who have no
feelings. For a week I was in Salzburg alone . . . it was
raining and cold . . . I had no overcoat! I was unhappy
. . . and I thought you were in the family . . . you
would understand. . . . Well, I was mistaken. . . ."
We were by then melted to tears and as contrite as if
we had indeed committed some outrageous sin. We said
we were sorry—if we had only known. At last he was

mollified. "But if you do such a thing again," he warned us as he turned his head to face the road, "I will never speak to you again! *Mai* . . . Never! Never!"

The Toscaninis moved into a villa in Liefering, a village some miles from town, and into it also moved their daughters, Wanda Horowitz and Wally Castelbarco, with their husbands and a small child apiece, also Mrs. Toscanini's sister and brother-in-law, the Polos. My wife and I rented a room in a farmhouse near by, but we took our meals with the Toscaninis. Each morning around ten the Maestro would pick us up in his car on his way to rehearsal in the town. *Die Meistersinger* was being prepared. The artists sat in a semicircle around the Maestro. They sang their roles to the accompaniment of a piano played by Erich Leinsdorf (now conductor of the Rochester Philharmonic), with the Maestro beating out the time by clapping his hands. The cast, which consisted of celebrated and experienced artists, might have been a group of beginners learning their parts, so unrelenting was the Maestro's beat and so intent was he on their being letter-perfect as to the duration of notes, nuances, and phrasing. This classwork went on daily for a fortnight, after which the rehearsals, now with orchestra and stage directions, were transferred to the opera house.

Only a week before the first performance we became aware that all was not going well with the production of *Die Meistersinger*. At home, in the evenings, the Maestro looked melancholy, ate sparingly, and often put his head in his hands and softly murmured to himself: "*Povero* Toscanini . . . *Povero* Toscanini." At last, one night, he spoke out. He was unhappy about one of the leading members of the cast. "He is a good man . . . a good artist . . . but not for this role," he said. "But you yourself chose him," I protested. "Besides, it's too late now. He came here at great expense, rented a villa, and brought his family. You can't send him away now. It would ruin his reputation." The Maestro shot me a look of scorn. "Are you asking me to think to this man or to think to Wagner?" My heart ached for "this man." But the Maestro had scored a point, and any appeal to sentiment would be regarded as an affront to his integrity as an artist. We telephoned to Munich for an acceptable replacement and, finding one, spent half the night composing a letter to "this man." The gist of it was that the Maestro had noticed at rehearsals that the artist was not well. Should the artist decide to leave the cast and go away for a cure, the Maestro would quite understand, and so forth. A reply arrived the following day. The artist thanked the Maestro for his solicitude. It was quite true that he was unwell. He would avail himself of the Maestro's kind suggestion to leave the cast and go somewhere for a cure, and so forth.

The whole Toscanini household was saddened by this episode. But after a satisfactory rehearsal with the replacement from Munich, the Maestro brightened up. A few days later there was a never-to-be-forgotten dress rehearsal of *Die Meistersinger* when the Maestro drove orchestra, chorus, and principals to such emotional heights that when the curtain fell and was then permanently raised for criticism and last-minute touches, as is customary at dress rehearsals, no one on the crowded stage stirred, but all stood frozen like effigies, their eyes tear-dimmed. The Maestro, too, stood for a while stockstill in the pit, his left hand on his hip, his right covering his eyes. He, too, was moved. Altogether forgotten was the poor man who had sacrificially betaken himself to a "cure." Wagner had been superbly "thought to" at the cost of one individual's happiness—and who could say that it was not justified?

The rehearsals for *Falstaff* were not less exciting. There were, fortunately, no replacements. But one incident nearly canceled its presentation. On a certain morning we repaired to the theater to see the sets for *Falstaff* mounted for the first time on the stage. All was well until the curtain went up on the interior of Mr. Ford's house. After one look the Maestro rose from his seat and rushed for the door. The scene-painter, the director, and other dignitaries ran up to him to find the cause of his displeasure. "*Vergogna!* [Shame!]" the Maestro cried, including with a great sweep of his hand the theater and everyone in it in his stricture. "Do you call *that*"—pointing to the offending scene on the stage— "an Elizabethan house! You know no-*thing*, no-*thing*. Go read what Verdi says in the score! No! This is not a theater. It is a place for the *ignoranti!* I will not conduct in such a place. . . . No! No! Never . . . never!" His hoarse voice rose to a scream, drowning out the frightened, protesting "buts" of the designer and *régisseur*. I ran into the street to shoo away the photographers who were always lying in wait to snap the Maestro. One of them had set up his camera on a tripod in front of the motor car at the stage-door entrance. I begged him to leave and told him about the Maestro's belligerent state of mind. He would not be budged. He had been sent by some international news service to get a picture of Toscanini and told not to come back without one. The Maestro was coming through the stage door, his wife behind him. I tore off my jacket and threw it over his head, and pushed him from the rear toward his automobile. Emilio, sensing his big moment, had already started his engine. As soon as we were in the car, he drove straight toward the cameraman as if to run him down. In his haste to avoid what seemed like certain disaster the cameraman tripped and caught his foot in the tripod, and camera, tripod, and man crashed noisily to the street as Emilio deftly steered his car away. I removed my jacket from the Maestro's head. Understanding the necessity for my action, he had not lifted a hand to remove it himself. Emilio, knowing by long experience what to do, headed for the open country. For an hour we drove in complete silence. When we returned to the Toscanini villa we found an elaborately worded message from the Salzburg Intendant that a new set in the authentic Elizabethan style had already been started and would be ready on the morrow for the Maestro's inspection.

When, on the following day, the curtain went up on the new interior of Ford's house the Maestro said triumphantly: "*Ecco!* [There it is]." *Falstaff* gave no further real trouble. A minor flurry developed when the romantic young couple in the opera failed to steal the prescribed furtive kisses in the Ford garden in time with the rapid tempo of the music. The Maestro shouted: "No! No!" climbed up onto the stage, pushed the tenor aside, and nimbly planted rapid kisses on the ingénue soprano's lips. "So!" he shouted. "Like this!" After several tries, the kissing was accomplished to the Maestro's satisfaction. At last the opera seemed prepared to perfection. Yet at every performance, in the intermission before the last act, the Maestro called the principals to his dressing-room and painstakingly rehearsed them in the final fugue. "You know, singers forget quickly," he said each time in explanation.

The Maestro had little privacy in his villa at Liefering. The Toscanini children, their wives and husbands, *their* children with their nurses, the uncle and aunt and *their* daughter and her husband, and numerous friends and friends of friends turned the place into a kind of Italian *pensione*, gay and noisy and uninhibited. Except at those times when some rehearsal or performance "poison-ed," as he claimed, the Maestro's life, the inmates, including *"Papá,"* behaved like any outsize Italian middle-class family. Children screamed and laughed, everybody talked at the same time, the voices trying to outdo each other in pitch and emphasis, often rising to what sounded to non-Italian ears like alarming belligerence. (Actually the subject matter always turned out to be inconsequential. One such verbal free-for-all that I nervously expected to end in blows proved to be an animated discussion about a dress Mrs. Toscanini thought she had sent to the cleaners, but which happily turned up the next day in the Signora's bedroom closet.)

In the afternoons, friends would arrive with movie cameras and someone would whip up a little scenario in which the entire family would act. The Maestro played ball with his grandchildren as the cameras ground away, or acted the hero or villain of a grotesque scenario with the emphasis on facial grimaces, bodily posturings, and buttock-slapping.

The Maestro's hearty willingness to be photographed by his family and friends and his refusal to pose for the press brought frustration and despair to the publicity department of the Salzburg Festival. However, his mere presence at the opera house was sufficient to insure the success of the season. Mainly because of him, the picturesque town was crammed with people of all nationalities running around in leather pants or dirndls. Tickets for the Toscanini performances were at an extravagant premium, and Josef, the factotum of the Österreichischer Hof (the town's best hotel), made a fortune from rich Americans who were willing to pay anything for the coveted tickets. Crowds followed the Maestro's Cadillac. He dared not show his face on the street for fear of being mobbed, and only in the country could he feel free to walk about.

One night after a late rehearsal, he was prevailed upon to visit an inconspicuous restaurant in the town, where there would be little likelihood of his being recognized. But we miscalculated, for his appearance threw the shabby place into an uproar. The crowded, chattering room suddenly grew silent; the proprietor ran toward us, quite beside himself as to how to make us welcome. "What an honor, *Herr Maestro*," he kept repeating as he bowed low to the ground, at the same time waving his arms backward in an effort to spur the gaping waitress into action. When we were finally seated, he ran off, and a moment later returned with a bottle of wine. This bottle, he assured the Maestro, was his special stock, and he wished to have the great honor of the great Maestro's opinion on it. The place was not of a kind to inspire confidence in the quality of its fare. I thought it prudent to taste the wine first, and when I did so my skepticism was fully justified. Never had I tasted a liquid so raw and sharp and rancid. I leaned toward the Maestro and whispered in English: "For God's sake, don't touch it. It's terrible." The proprietor had filled the Maestro's glass to the brim and now stood by anxiously awaiting the verdict. To my horror, the Maestro lifted his glass, said *"Salute"* to his host, and stoically downed the vile concoction to the last drop. A spasm of distaste screwed up his face for a second. The next moment he smiled and put down his empty glass. *"Buono, buono,"* he said. "*Grazie* . . . *grazie*." The beaming host refilled the glass and the Maestro, after a pause, drank it down. Of course, the rest of us felt obliged to follow suit. To forestall the host's further pressure and the Maestro's gallant acquiescence, I pointed to the lateness of the hour, and our party, greatly relieved, rose to go. On the way home I asked the Maestro why he hadn't heeded my warning about the wine. He gave me a reproachful look. "He was so kind. I could not be rude," he said.

Yet the very next week he proved that he could quite easily be remarkably rude. There was a lunch at his villa, and among his invited guests was old Frau Thode, Richard Wagner's stepdaughter and granddaughter of Franz Liszt. Ever since she had met the Maestro at Bayreuth she had adored him as the greatest interpreter of Wagner's music she had ever heard. I sat next to her at lunch. There was much talk of Wagner and *Die Meistersinger*, which the Maestro had conducted the night before. To please Frau Thode, I steered the conversation to the music of her grandfather, Franz Liszt. At the mention of Liszt the Maestro's face grew dark. "Don't speak to me of Liszt," he said. I was astonished and mortified. I admired Liszt and had thought the Maestro did too. At any rate, I felt he should have spared the sensibilities of Liszt's granddaughter. I tried to change the subject, but the Maestro went on bitterly about Liszt. "He was a charlatan," he proclaimed, looking pointedly at Frau Thode as if she was directly implicated in her grandfather's perfidy. "He was a *poseur*, and his music is insincere." Frau Thode pressed my hand in anguish, and her eyes filled with tears. I rushed to Liszt's defense, but I could not prevail over the Maestro's blazing eyes and scornful invective. When I saw that my efforts only drove him to a more virulent attack, I decided to ease Frau Thode's situation by distracting the Maestro suddenly. I knew he despised Mascagni. He had often inveighed against him and his music. "Maestro," I said, "why is it that I like *Cavalleria Rusticana* so much? I know it is not a great work, but it has a power—" The switch from Liszt to Mascagni was instantaneous, like a montage in a movie. "Why?" the Maestro yelled at me. "Why you like *Cavalleria?* I tell you why. Because you are *stupido . . . ignorante . . .* that is why . . . *Dio . . . Madonna . . . Santissima . . .*" He was off on Mascagni, on Leoncavallo, on the whole Italian *verismo* school—"*degenerato.*" Everybody at the table saw the trick and felt relieved. Frau Thode dried her eyes with her handkerchief and pressed my hand in gratitude. The crisis was over.

I often thought that the Maestro's temperament resembled the Salzburg weather, which was kaleidoscopic in its changes. Without warning it would rain, black clouds would hasten through the sky, thunder would roll ominously close. Then suddenly the rain would cease and a bright sun would sop up every bit of moisture, the green landscape would shine pleasantly, as if it had always shone like that, and the distant mountains would come closer to the town, their milky transparency as immediate as if seen through a telescope. Toscanini, too, presented in a single day transformations without number. He was naïve, crafty, simple, complex, kind, and ferociously spiteful. The moods *inhabited* him without forewarning, and evaporated as mysteriously.

He was most appealing when a prey to a quiet, gentle sadness. When on our last day in Salzburg we came to bid him good-by, he appeared moved, and he embraced us gently. "We shall probably never meet again," he said. He had left the Philharmonic and America for good that spring.

"Oh, yes, we shall," I said optimistically. "If you won't come to America, we'll come to Italy."

He shook his head. "No! I am sixty-nine. . . . I am old . . . too old . . . it is time to die. . . . V*a*, *vecchio* John!" ("Go, aged John," quoted from *Falstaff.*) He looked old at the moment. His words, I thought, could be prophetic.

CHAPTER FOUR

$\mathcal{I}$N the fall of 1936, at a dinner party in New York, I met General David Sarnoff, then president of the Radio Corporation of America and chairman of the board of the National Broadcasting Company. We talked about music and discovered in each other an admiration for the great voices of the past, a brash addiction to melody, and a reverence for the art of Arturo Toscanini. "What a pity," I said, "that America will never hear and see the Maestro again." He agreed that it was a pity, and thought something should be done about it.

Several weeks later I met Mr. Sarnoff at a concert. He gave me a lift in his car; as we drove along, he suddenly offered me a job at NBC. I told him I knew nothing about radio and asked him what kind of job he had in mind. He said he hadn't the faintest idea, but would I please talk to Mr. John Royal, in charge of programs at NBC. I thought the offer rather strange, but

when I got to know Mr. Sarnoff better, I understood that
I was one of his hunches. And, while it was perfectly true
that at the moment he didn't know just what to do with
me at NBC, he was, so to speak, putting me on ice for
the time when his hunch would take concrete shape. So
I took a part-time job at NBC with duties as nebulous as
a court favorite's.

In due time the hunch materialized. Mr. Sarnoff
called me to his office one day and told me he had made
up his mind to persuade Toscanini to return to America.
I could not help smiling in pity for his ignorance of Toscanini's character. "He will never come back," I said.
"He told me so himself." I sketched for Mr. Sarnoff a
verbal portrait of the Maestro, underscoring his absolute
intransigence. I pointed out that once the Maestro made
up his mind about something, he could not be budged.
When he left the Metropolitan in 1915, for example,
Otto Kahn, the opera house's Mæcenas, moved heaven
and earth to get him to return. He finally dispatched a
cable to Milan begging the Maestro to come back on his
own terms as to fees, rehearsals, artists, and anything else
he thought important. The Maestro had not even
deigned to reply.

My disclosures failed to disturb Mr. Sarnoff. "We'll
try," he said amiably, and I told him to remember that I
had warned him. I was then commanded to send the
Maestro a cable offering him a cross-country tour with
the Philadelphia Orchestra, to be sponsored by RCA
Victor, the recording company under RCA's banner. To

this the Maestro promptly replied: "Thank you dear friend no. Arturo Toscanini." Disappointed but triumphant, I showed the cable to Mr. Sarnoff, who read it without emotion and said: "Let's think up something else." I could think of nothing else. "Suppose," he went on calmly, "we offered to *create* an orchestra for him—a *radio* orchestra. Would he go for that?" I shook my head pityingly. No. I was certain he would not. He had no interest in radio. His Sunday matinees with the Philharmonic Symphony were broadcast, but for him they were just concerts. Radio was mechanical, like recording. For many years he had refused all offers to record. He would refuse to be primarily a radio conductor.

"Very well," said Mr. Sarnoff. "I want you to go to Milan and get him. The American radio listener deserves the very best in music. All we can lose is a few weeks of your time and the expenses of the trip. No more cables. Get on a boat."

However, I did send one last cable in which I told the Maestro I expected to be in Milan early in February and hoped I could see him. He smelled a rat. "Think to my age!" he cabled back.

Believing that I might at some point require feminine co-operation, I took my wife along. The voyage was a stormy one, and I spent most of it in bed alternately dozing and dipping into the books and magazines friends had sent to the boat. In one of the magazines my jaundiced attention was caught by an article on canaries. I am ordinarily indifferent to canaries, but the paragraph

that caught my eye recounted the behavior of a flock of
canaries in the author's living-room during a Philharmonic Symphony Sunday broadcast of Beethoven's
Ninth Symphony, conducted by Toscanini. During the
first three movements, said the article, the canaries were
silent. But at the entrance of the chorus in the finale, the
birds settled themselves on the radio console and sang
along. This amused me. Hoping it might also amuse Toscanini, I shoved the magazine into a valise for possible
future use.

We arrived in Milan late on a piercingly cold,
snowy afternoon and went to the hotel Principe e Savoia,
close to the railroad station. So certain was I that my
mission would fail that I at once made inquiries about a
return passage within a week. Then I telephoned Mrs.
Toscanini. She said the Maestro was in one of his somber moods, and that she would be right over. Half an
hour later she was in our room. It was obvious that she
wished to warn us about the Maestro's current state of
unreceptiveness toward whatever scheme we had in
mind. Our room being ice cold, Mrs. Toscanini suggested that we all get into bed and continue our conversation in a less frigid temperature. The three of us
piled into bed and pulled the feather comforter up to our
necks. In that supine position I disclosed the purpose of
my visit. My wife, who spoke Italian, was my interpreter.
(Although Mrs. Toscanini had spent years in America,
she spoke no English, a circumstance that her husband
attributed to her stubborn provincialism.) Almost from

the start she began shaking her head and muttering: "No, no . . . *impossible* . . . *mai!*"—a reaction I had fully expected. Indeed, what with my deep-rooted pessimism about the project, the piercing cold, the dreary, wet aspect of the city from our bedroom window, and the prospect of facing the ill-disposed Toscanini, I would gladly have seized our still unpacked valises and fled Italy, if that had been possible.

After an hour's conversation in bed, Mrs. Toscanini said it was time for her to go home. She would expect us for dinner that night. She had no objection to my broaching the project to the Maestro, though I must have no illusions about his answer. Perhaps, she said, I had better wait for some more propitious moment. I grasped at the possibility of a respite.

Later, in the Via Durini, we found the Maestro indeed in a somber mood. His greeting lacked even a hint of the old warmth. The conversation at table was strained. Several times I was on the point of making a clean breast of it. Reconciled to the expected refusal, I was prepared for a quick farewell and an immediate return to America. But courage failed me, and we returned dispirited to our icy bedroom in the hotel. The next morning Mrs. Toscanini telephoned that we were to lunch and dine with them during our stay in Milan. Dutifully but hopelessly we drove twice a day to the Via Durini. Some meals went better than others, but none gave me an opening. The Maestro spoke little. When he did speak, it was mostly bitter invective against Mussolini and what he called his *ladri* (thieves), and the misfortunes they had brought on Italy.

One day the Toscaninis took us to lunch in a very large restaurant in the Galeria. This great, high, glass-roofed section of the city was more crowded than usual: the Fascists were celebrating something or other and Mussolini and Ciano had come to Milan for the festivities. Flags and streamers hung from windows, and the city had a holiday aspect. The restaurant was full. As we entered, all eyes turned to the Maestro. He was, as usual, oblivious of the sensation he was creating, but Mrs. Toscanini looked nervous. Although the Maestro was a popular figure, Milan was a Fascist stronghold and there was always the chance that some hothead might start a demonstration against the anti-Fascist conductor.

When we finished our lunch I made an attempt at conversation by describing our recent sea voyage. The Maestro asked me if our ship had called at Naples or had gone direct to Genoa. I told him we had stopped a day at Naples and were surprised at the change in the city since we had last seen it. "Mussolini certainly cleaned up Naples," I said thoughtlessly. I had hardly finished speaking when the Maestro screamed at me: "Mussolini! Do not speak of that *assassino!* That *porco!* I wish to kill him. I would be happy to kill him. . . ." He ranted on in Italian and in English for what seemed an eternity. I looked around me. Not a soul *appeared* to hear the Maestro. No one was looking our way. It was as if the Maestro were speaking in a language none of the diners understood or cared to understand. Mrs. Toscanini kept murmuring: *"Basta! Basta!* [enough, enough] *Papá,"* and clutching my hand in despair. He talked himself out at last. His wife hurriedly called for the bill, and we left the restaurant. For the first time I understood why Mussolini suffered his archenemy to go unmolested. I had seen the people in that restaurant *protecting* their beloved Toscanini by pretending to be deaf.

Two weeks went by and I had said nothing. Then the Maestro began to show restiveness at my strange reluctance to say what I had come for. I was sure that Mrs. Toscanini had not betrayed my confidence, for sometimes I would find him giving her sharp looks that said plainly: "Do you know anything? Why don't they speak?" His increasing irritation at meals and in the evenings did not loosen my tongue. It had, in fact, the opposite effect. And as the days passed slowly, the very faint hope of success that I might have secretly cherished vanished. I was waiting for an opening that seemed never to come. But always I took along with me the copy of the provocative magazine article on canaries, and a slip of paper on which I had outlined several different offers for a series of broadcasts with a future NBC Radio Orchestra. Not that I really expected ever to produce these documents. I only wanted to be prepared, in the unlikely event that I should need them.

At the end of this fruitless and depressing fortnight in Milan, the tension in the Toscanini apartment suddenly began to ease. One night we found two other guests at dinner—Mr. and Mrs. Giulio Gatti-Casazza. Gatti (as everybody called him) had just retired as general manager of the Metropolitan Opera Association and had returned (like Toscanini) to spend his declining years in his native land. Impresario and conductor had had a long association, both amicable and warring, in Italy and America. They appeared pleased to see each other, and their reminiscences of their colorful past continued throughout a lengthy dinner. It was a succession of humorous or dramatic experiences prefaced by "You recall, Gatti?" or "Maestro, it remembers me . . ." (They spoke English for my benefit, the Maestro fluently though rather archaically, Gatti with great difficulty and with abrupt excursions into Italian.) They recalled their first years together at La Scala, and how after a performance they would remain at the opera house until dawn, planning new productions and analyzing the merits and defects of the old ones. The faces of the two aging men reflected the bitter-sweet pleasure their recollections (and some excellent wine) induced.

"Do you remember, Gatti . . ." the Maestro said, and his face was suddenly clouded with some disturbing memory, "do you remember the *jettattore?*"

Gatti nodded his large head. "I remember well!" he said solemnly.

I looked perplexed, and the Maestro explained that a *jettattore* was a man who had the evil eye. "This poor man—Giovanni was his name—eh, Gatti?" Gatti nodded. "Si—Giovanni." "This Giovanni ruined my

first performance of Weber's *Euryanthe*. *Vero*, Gatti?"
Gatti nodded. "*Vero!*" he said. I was eager to hear how
the man with the evil eye ruined the *première* of *Euryanthe* in Italy. The Maestro turned to me. "Everybody
was afraid of Giovanni. . . ." ("*Naturalmente*," Gatti
put in.) "I, too. When I see him in the street I go the
other way." ("*Certo!*" Gatti murmured.) "Giovanni
was a good man. *Poveretto!* He could not help it to have
the evil eye. Think! He even married and had children!
Well, well! I was going to conduct *Euryanthe*. It was
the first time the opera would be given in Italy, and I had
many rehearsals. Many. *Vero*, Gatti? At last I was satis-
fi-ed. The theater had been sold out. *Vero*, Gatti? People
were coming from all over Italy to hear it, even from
Germany. Well, came the night of the performance. I
put on my frock and I go to La Scala. As I reach the
stage door I hear a voice from the other side of the street.
The voice say '*Buona sera*, Maestro.' My blood freeze. It
is the voice of the *jettattore*, Giovanni. I stay still. I pretend I do not hear. Shall I go in the theater or go home?
I did not know what to do. Then, of a sooden Giovanni
cross-ed over and came close to me. He put his hand out
to me so"—the Maestro stuck out a hand toward me—
"and he say-ed again: '*Buona sera*, Maestro.' Imagine
how I felt! But I could not deny to take his hand. *Povero*
me! I took it! Then I went sadly into the theater. Ah! I
think to me, what will now become of *Euryanthe!* It will
be a fiasco. Giovanni has put the evil eye on me. I was
disturb-ed. You remember, Gatti, I said to you: 'Gatti,

what shall we do? Shall we postpone the opera?' And you said: 'Too late, the people are all here, the opera must go on. We must take the chance.' *È vero*, Gatti? So I go before my orchestra, but without heart, without spirit. I begin the overture. To my surprise, the orchestra play no bad. They play, they play, they play, and it is no bad. It go well, very well. I am a-stoni-ed. I say to myself: 'Ah, Giovanni, you have lost your power. Your evil eye is no-*thing* no more. You can do no-*thing*.' The orchestra play better and better, eh, Gatti? And I finish the overture, and the people all scream: 'Bravo, bravo!' I am content. I laugh to myself. No more shall I be afraid of Giovanni. But wait! *Aspetta . . . aspetta . . .*" The Maestro had risen from his chair. His face was flushed. He waved his arms at me as if to caution me against optimism.

"The people scream: 'Bravo!' That is good. But they do not stop. I wait for silence to begin the opera. They do not stop. For five, for ten minutes they scream. I do nothing. I stand with my back and wait. They will not let me begin the opera. You must understand I never permit *bis* [encore] at La Scala. *Mai*. Never. The people in Milan know I never permit *bis*. And now at last I understand. The *jettattore!* Giovanni! The evil eye! It had worked. Giovanni had won. The people scream: '*Bis . . . bis!*' I turn around. 'No *bis!*' I scream back, and I break the baton in half and throw the pieces at them. Then I go home to bed. *Vero*, Gatti?" Gatti now took over and related how the *première* was postponed to the following week, when the Maestro and everybody at the

Scala took special precautions to avoid the *jettattore*. And, having steered clear of the baleful Giovanni, the performance went on without interruption and became the season's greatest success.

The Gattis left. I stayed on purposely. I had suddenly decided that the moment had arrived for me to talk to the Maestro. The visit of the Gattis, the old memories, and perhaps the wine had put the Maestro off his guard. He was amiable and talkative. He urged me to have some brandy. He had poured some out for himself and applied a match to a lump of sugar, an invariable indication of good temper. His face glowed with satisfaction as the blue flames spilled over the glass. Now, if ever, was the moment! I must have had a great deal to drink, for, strangely enough, my fears had vanished. I attacked the subject boldly, without preliminaries. I said that all America was hoping for his return. I told him it was useless for him to talk about his being old. He was younger, in spirit, yes, in physical stamina, too, than any other conductor in the world. The NBC would build him a great orchestra. Instead of being played to a few thousand people in Carnegie Hall, his music would reach millions over the radio. I did not let him interrupt. I talked eloquently without pausing for a second. I advanced all the arguments I had been marshaling in my mind for an occasion like this. I anticipated his objections. He stared at me incredulously as I spoke. My wife, too, looked at me in surprise, and so did Mrs. Toscanini.

But I needed a climax, a fortissimo finish. It suddenly came to me. I remembered the magazine article about the canaries. Had I forgotten to take it along? I felt in my pocket. It was there. "Maestro," I said, "did you know that canaries once sang the chorus of the Ninth Symphony? Well, they did!" And before he could speak, I whipped out the magazine and read him the significant paragraph. He listened with mounting excitement. And when I finished he seized the magazine and read it for himself, holding the paper very close to his eyes and underlining the words with his forefinger. "*Senta,* Carla!" he cried to his wife, waving the article in her face. He was beside himself with excitement, and he poured out a stream of Italian, fiery and rapid, in his eagerness to impart to her the news of the miracle of the canaries in Cincinnati. Her wondering "No, Tosca! *Impossibile!*" only heightened his fervor. I heard the words *uccelli* (birds), *Chin-chin-nati, rah-dio,* and *Novanta sinfonia* (Ninth Symphony) with pleasure, and I gathered by the rapid flow of his speech and his vivid gestures that, carried away by his own enthusiasm, he was heightening and elaborating the printed story. At last he stopped, apparently on a triumphant note, for Mrs. Toscanini murmured: "*Incredibile . . . meraviglia.*"

My moment had arrived. "Maestro," I said, taking his hand, "this is one of the marvels of radio. It is touching to know that canaries can be excited into song by the Ninth Symphony played a thousand miles away. But think of the millions of people who will also hear it and be touched and comforted by it . . . millions of people on farms and in little villages who have never heard a live symphony orchestra and never can. And when your music goes over the air," I continued shrewdly, "everyone who hears will know the way the composer *meant* the music to be played, they will hear the difference between your revelation of what Beethoven and Mozart and Haydn and Wagner *intended* and the dreadful misrepresentations of second-class conductors which they call 'interpretations.' Maestro, *will* you come?" There was a pause that seemed an eternity. Toscanini's eyes were probing me like an X-ray, as if to make completely sure of my veracity. Then he looked away and dropped the words "Why not!" like a bombshell in the oppressive silence.

I was taken aback. The situation seemed quite unreal. I needed a moment for recovery. But if what I'd heard was really true, I must leave nothing in doubt, but must clinch the matter then and there. I extracted from my pocketbook a paper that contained the National Broadcasting Company's three separate offers to the Maestro, one for ten broadcasts, one for fifteen, and one for twenty. I handed the paper to him, saying: "Which of these do you like?" He scrutinized the offers carefully and pointed to the first. Mrs. Toscanini, who had behaved with complete impartiality, was suddenly presented with a *fait accompli*. Now she turned her attention to the practical aspects of the engagement. She took the paper from her husband, asked him some questions, and then said to me in studied English, pausing between

the words: "*You*—pay—income—tass." Too excited at
the moment to calculate what that additional burden
might amount to, and quite forgetting my obligation to
the company I worked for, I said rashly: "Yes, yes, of
course. Signora, may I use your telephone? I want to tell
the great news to Mr. Sarnoff." A look of apprehension
passed over Mrs. Toscanini's face. "Telephone to
America?" she asked severely. I hastened to set her mind
at rest. "*I* pay for telephone," I assured her. "*NBC* pay."
She looked relieved. "N.B.Chile pay," she laughed, making the name sound like the Italian equivalent of "im-
becile." She liked her little joke, and we laughed with,
her.

Mr. Sarnoff was delighted with the success of my
mission and congratulated me warmly. "And what do I
do now?" I asked him. He replied: "Sign him up." I told
him I had never signed anybody up, and would not know
how to go about doing such a thing. He said he would
leave that to me, and so terminated the costly transatlantic conversation, much to Mrs. Toscanini's relief. Although certain that NBC would foot the bill, she disapproved of extravagance in general. Actually she was the
most generous of women, helping the sick and needy,
sending underprivileged children to the country in the
summer, finding jobs for people, and supporting desti-
tute friends and relatives for years if need be. It was the
small sums that bothered her. Thus, in the mistaken
belief that she was economizing, she would travel miles,
using up a dollar's worth of gasoline, to buy one pound

of butter cheaper than she could buy it in a shop nearer home.

I told the Maestro that American business firms insisted on certain routine, impersonal documents such as contracts, and he said he quite understood, that he had once, a long time ago, signed such a document, and would not mind signing another for me. So I borrowed a decrepit typewriter from a friendly neighbor, and on a single sheet of paper I typed three or four paragraphs stating the simple facts of our agreement. This the Maestro cheerfully signed without reading. Although he and his wife and my wife and I were the only persons in Milan who knew the terms of the contract, the *Corriere della Sera*, the city's leading newspaper, carried a story the following morning which told in full detail about my visit, its purpose, its success, and the number of broadcasts and the fee. The Maestro explained with bitterness that the Fascists made it their business to find out everything pertaining to him, and that his telephone was always tapped.

The night before we left for America I gave a dinner at Savini's, the town's best restaurant, to the Toscaninis and a few of their relatives. We drank toasts to one another, to Mr. Sarnoff, and to NBC. Then we went on to the Manzoni Theater, where the Maestro had taken a box. The play was Pirandello's *Six Characters in Search of an Author*. The performance was given in memory of Pirandello, who had recently died, and before the start of the play a man came onto the stage and made a long memorial speech. The Maestro, refusing to sit down, took up a position in the rear of the box. He was at once spotted. People nudged each other and pointed to him, and hundreds of opera glasses were trained on him. The man on the stage, judging by his theatrical gestures and rising voice, was making a significant point, when from behind me the Maestro spoke out loud and sarcastically. I couldn't understand what he was saying. But it was clear that he did not agree with what the man was saying, and was voicing his dissent. In a like vein, the Maestro kept up a loud, running commentary during the course of the play. Such behavior in theaters was not uncommon in Italy. I had heard people at La Scala hiss and boo and advise artists who had incurred their displeasure to leave the stage and abjure their profession forever. But that so public a figure as Toscanini would avail himself of a common privilege that could only achieve what he most dreaded—calling attention to himself—was a mystery indeed. The only possible explanation was the Maestro's naïve unawareness of his eminence and importance. He thought of himself as an anonymous member of the audience, and therefore behaved like one.

Returning to New York, I started at once to put together an orchestra that would be worthy of Toscanini. Symphony orchestras are not built in a day, and we had only ten months in which to assemble one before the Maestro's first broadcast on Christmas night 1937. We had engaged Artur Rodzinski as assistant conductor, and he and I now desperately attempted to make up for the time we didn't have by signing up the very best men available. The best men were not always available, but I did everything possible—rather unscrupulously, I must own—to wean them away from other orchestras. We were asked to pay unheard-of salaries to first-desk men, and we agreed to pay them. And so unequivocal was my belief in the crusading nature of Toscanini's return to America that I assumed that all the other conductors of our symphony orchestras would be as concerned for its success as I was. It was under some such quixotic misapprehension that I called on a famous conductor to release his first bass-player to the Toscanini orchestra. Nor could I then understand the conductor's polite but firm refusal to cripple his own orchestra.

Mr. Rodzinski and I gave innumerable auditions to applicants, and at last I was able to write the Maestro that the orchestra had been tentatively formed. I enclosed a list of the players I would, with his approval, engage. Promptly the Maestro returned the list, but he had put crosses next to many names and had made revealing notations in parentheses underneath: "Be careful, he drinks!" "His intonation is bad." "He is not a good musician." Of course I went into the charges thoroughly. The alleged toper we were fortunately able to keep. For, while the Maestro's memory proved to be historically accurate—the man confessed that he had been too free with the bottle fifteen years earlier, when he had played at La Scala—he had long since taken the pledge. As for the man whose intonation was bad and the one who was not a good musician, there was nothing for us to do but heed the Maestro's warning: they were not engaged.

We were now in the last week of November. Everything was ready. We had assembled a superb body of men. They were being whipped into shape by the severe and meticulous Rodzinski. The country was in a high state of anticipation. The National Broadcasting Company had already spent a young fortune in the creation of the orchestra and in its administration. Pending the final seal of the Maestro's approval upon his arrival, I luxuriated in the realization of an impossible dream and the completion of a difficult job.

From this state of euphoria I was rudely jolted one morning at breakfast by a cable from the Maestro. "I have received news unpleasant," it read, "that because of the high cost of the new orchestra and myself the NBC is causing some of its employees to lose their jobs. This I do not like. Please release me from my contract. I stay in Italy. Arturo Toscanini."

I was dismayed. While I could make no sense out of the message, I realized that, whatever the misunderstanding on the Maestro's part, we might not be able to clear it up in time for the scheduled opening of our season. I hastened to Mr. Sarnoff's office with the cable and we discussed what measures to take. One of the Maestro's daughters, the Countess Castelbarco, was in New York, and we telephoned her to join us. She was as mystified by the cable as we were. Mr. Sarnoff suggested that she talk with her father on the transatlantic telephone. But when the connection with Milan came through, it was her mother who answered. The Countess, on the verge of hysteria, talked to her mother in Italian for a long time. When she hung up, she told us that her father had refused to speak to her. He had been terribly upset by the arrival of an anonymous cable, and he had sworn that he would not be the cause of anyone's losing his job, and would therefore refuse to come to America. His decision, her mother told her, was unalterable. The Countess, wiping away her tears, concluded ominously: "You know Father!"

As a last resort I decided to make a personal appeal to the Maestro, and after many tries I wrote out a long cable calculated to melt a heart of stone. If that failed, we would have to accept defeat and start undoing the labor of many months. I wired that, far from causing one man to lose his job at NBC, his engagement had led the company to take on, besides a full symphony orchestra, a number of people to meet the increased demands of the engineering, publicity, and press departments. I begged him to remember that in our many years of friendship I had never misrepresented anything to him. And I earnestly asked him to consider whether he was justified in believing some anonymous troublemaker and questioning my veracity. I ended by swearing that my only concern was to serve the cause of music, as I believed his to be.

Day after day we waited, and no reply came. During this time the Countess spoke frequently to her mother by telephone. It appeared that my cable had not altered the Maestro's decision, except that his outbursts against me and the NBC had subsided. Several days later Mrs. Toscanini was able to report to her daughter that *Papá* was now *calmo*. This in itself was hopeful, but hardly enough to dispel my fears. For a fortnight the fate of the orchestra and the broadcasts hung on a word from the Via Durini. At last, when I had given up hope, there came a terse wire from the Maestro naming the date of his departure for America on the *Île de France*. The long tension was over, yet I could not rid myself of an uneasy feeling that something more might occur to keep the Maestro from our shores. Each morning I half expected to find an ominous cable on my breakfast tray. Nor was I able to relax until we received word from our Paris office that the *Île de France* had sailed with the Maestro and his wife aboard.

The Maestro's arrival posed the ever-recurring problem of keeping press photographers away from him. Whatever influence the NBC Press Department brought to bear on the editors and reporters of the city's newspapers resulted only in vague promises not to use flashbulbs, provided we could get the Maestro to pose on deck, where the natural light would be sufficient. At six o'clock on the morning of the arrival of the *Île de France*, along with a large contingent of newspapermen and women, I boarded a cutter and steamed out to the bay, where we lay around and waited for the liner. Soon she loomed through the fog and anchored, and we climbed aboard. I knocked at the Maestro's cabin. Mrs. Toscanini's voice asked: *"Chi e là?"* and when I shouted my name she unlocked the door. I went in and she locked it again. The Maestro's greeting was impersonal, not exactly friendly, rather reservedly polite, as if he still harbored a suspicion that I might have deceived him in the matter of the anonymous cable. Presently there was a knock at the door. It was the steward summoning Mr. and Mrs. Toscanini to the ship's lounge to have their passports stamped. I went with them, and we continued our conversation in the lounge. The American immigration officers had received instructions to give the Toscaninis priority, and a few minutes later their passports were stamped and we were headed back to the cabin.

At that moment a man with a camera materialized as if from nowhere and flashed a light bulb directly in the Maestro's face. The Maestro let out a piercing yell, clutched at his eyes, and then, screaming Italian maledictions, ran in pursuit of the fleeing cameraman. Through the door he ran and out onto the long deck, I after him, Mrs. Toscanini a poor fourth behind. The cameraman was very fleet, but the Maestro was steadily gaining on him when suddenly two nuns who were walking briskly toward the salon stood directly in his way. As the Maestro veered to one side to avoid the sisters, one of them put out a restraining hand and clutched at his sleeve. With an imprecation he jerked his arm free and sped on. But the momentary halt had given the cameraman time to disappear. I caught up with the Maestro at the end of the long deck, where he stood irresolute, baffled, fuming and gesticulating wildly. I led him back to his cabin, where he collapsed in a chair, the picture of utter desolation. By now the ship was being maneuvered into its berth. The steward reappeared and led us, by prearrangement, to a cabin in the tourist class, from where we disembarked quite unnoticed, while a host of photographers and newspapermen patiently waited for us at the first-class gangplank.

We got into a car that was waiting for us and drove to the Astor Hotel. The Maestro had by this time recovered from the effects of his sprint on deck, and appeared rather to enjoy our having given the press the slip. He looked unusually handsome as he sat in the back of the car, bolt upright, on his head a Breton beret at a jaunty angle, a long flannel scarf carelessly draped around his neck. Although it was a cold December morning, he had refused to put on his overcoat. Now he looked out of the window at the familiar New York scene with obvious pleasure. "I like New York," he said. "I always like-ed it. It is a living city . . . it is like strong wine." His high spirits emboldened me to put a question to him. "You gave us a bad time these last few weeks, Maestro," I began. "Why did you do it?" He turned his head to me in surprise. "Why? Because you make a man lose his job." I gasped. "But, Maestro, we did *not* make anyone lose his job. On the contrary, because of your coming we gave jobs to many." He looked at me sharply.

"You are *syou-*er?" he asked. I disdained to reply. He saw that he had hurt me, and hastened to change the subject. "And the or*ches*tra? How is it? You wrote me Silva no longer drink. Are you *syou-*er?"

The following morning I called to take him to his first rehearsal. A large dressing-room on the eighth floor of the NBC Studios had been fitted up for him. Mrs. Toscanini brought along a valise with his shirts, handkerchiefs, rehearsal coats, fans, a half-dozen framed photographs of members of his family, several little photographs of Verdi, one each of Brahms and Wagner, and a miniature of Beethoven. Wherever he conducted these pictures were set up in his dressing-room. I suspected that they were a part of his large collection of superstitions. At any rate, I had seen them in his dressing-room in Salzburg, in Bayreuth, and in Carnegie Hall. Mrs. Toscanini arranged the pictures on the piano, then assisted her husband in putting on his rehearsal jacket, a black alpaca garment with a clerical collar. She brushed his silky white hair toward the back of his head in a kind of cottontail effect. The Maestro sprayed his face and head with an atomizer containing his favorite toilet water. He then selected a baton from a number of sticks of various sizes and weights.

He was plainly nervous when I told him the orchestra was ready. As we were about to leave his room, he hastily took up from the bureau a small crucifix attached to a silver chain, and a set of tiny pictures reposing in a number of little metal frames resembling a segmented bracelet. These objects he first raised to his lips, then slipped into the pockets of his trousers. Silently we made our way through the long winding corridor that led from his room to Studio 8H, the NBC concert hall. As we reached the anteroom of the studio, we heard members of the orchestra tuning up, trying out their fingers or their lungs, and building up the usual atonal counterpoint of snatches from every variety of orchestral and instrumental composition. Suddenly there was silence, the kind of silence that is as blatant as the loudest noise. Not the sound of a breath, a scratch, a movement came to us from Studio 8H. I held open the swing door and said: "Ready, Maestro." He looked quite pale, as if he were a novice about to make his debut. His wife went up to him and kissed him on the forehead. At the door he stopped abruptly and held up his hands for a moment in prayer. I preceded him to the stage and called out in a voice that sounded strange to me: "Gentlemen . . . Maestro Toscanini." The men leaped to their feet, the string-players beat their stands with their bows. The Maestro bowed his head once, cut short the demonstration by motioning the men to their seats, rapped sharply with his baton on the stand nearest him, said in a hoarse voice: "Brahms," and the opening fateful rhythmic measures of the Brahms First Symphony cut the air. He played through the first movement without stopping. At the end he said: *"Non c'e male"* (not so bad) . Then resolutely, *"Da capo"* (from the beginning) , he sang out, and brought his right arm down sharply in a downbeat which he fortified with a hoarse "uh," and the re-hearsal was on in earnest. For one hour and a half he was on his feet, shouting, swearing, cajoling, his baton describing unorthodox convolutions, straight-up-and-down rapier stabs, delicate sideswipes, long horizontal even undulations like a gently-moving multi-arched snake, or sudden circular movements like a cowboy twirling a lariat. At last he stopped, took his watch from his pocket, held it very close to his eyes, and, realizing that he had overstepped the union regulation of an intermission after an hour of rehearsal, said contritely: "Excuse me," and stepped off the podium. His face and head were sopping wet, and beads of sweat gleamed at the tip of his nose. As we entered his dressing-room Mrs. Toscanini, in fur coat and hat, came in through another door. She had evidently spent the hour and a half shopping, and had arrived just in time to pretend she had not left the room. Never had I seen garments so wet as the rehearsal coat and undershirt we removed with difficulty. "You know," the Maestro said with pride, "I perspire water—pure water!" And, indeed, he spoke the truth. We rubbed him down with a coarse towel, which we then draped over his shoulders. His wife gave him a lozenge to chew, and a straw fan which he wielded vigorously over his scalp all through the quarter-hour of intermission. He seemed at ease, and I hazarded a question. "And the orchestra, Maestro?" I asked. He interrupted his fanning and said: "I am content." A moment later he stopped fanning himself again. "Send me Mischakoff," he said (Mischakoff was the concertmaster). I ran out and returned with Mischakoff. "*Caro* Mischakoff," the Maestro said, "do not make too much *vibrato* in the solo at the end of the Adagio. I beg of you, not too much *vibrato*. . . . Thank you, my dear. . . ." Mischakoff left and the Maestro leaned back in his chair, closed his eyes, and fanned himself mechanically. Now and again he raised his left hand and beat out a measure, or made undulating motions as if molding a phrase. I gazed at him with emotion. At this moment nothing in the world mattered to him but the contour of a phrase in the slow part of a Brahms symphony. In Studio 8H a perfect orchestra sat waiting and eager to realize his perfectionist's musical dream. In a few days every American possessing a radio would be able to share this dream. For the first time in nearly a year I could afford to relax. Certainly nothing could possibly occur between Wednesday morning and the following Saturday evening to prevent the opening broadcast on Christmas night. Yet I knew perfectly well that many things could happen. An anonymous telegram might arrive, a rehearsal might go awry, or the hapless *jettattore* Giovanni might suddenly appear at the stage door of Studio 8H and offer his baleful hand to the horrified Maestro. Agitated by these reflections, I sought comfort in my own superstitions and touched wood several times.

Eventually my fears proved to be unfounded. No anonymous wire arrived, the rehearsals pursued their exciting but non-catastrophic course, and no *jettattore* materialized at the stage entrance. The Christmas-night broadcast, played before a select and critical audience in the studio and heard over the radio by millions of people in the United States and Canada, took place without incident and to the Maestro's satisfaction.

CHAPTER FIVE

$\mathcal{F}$ROM 1937 to 1954, with the exception of one winter season, Toscanini led the NBC Symphony in history-making broadcasts, benefit concerts, and tours in the United States and South America. Until the outbreak of World War II in 1939, he spent the spring and early summer months in Italy, alternating between his house in the Via Durini in Milan and the villa on the Isolino San Giovanni in Lago Maggiore. In late summer he conducted concerts and opera in Salzburg, London, and Lucerne.

When in Italy, the Toscanini family lived in constant dread of Fascist reprisal, for Toscanini spoke his mind freely about the regime both at home and in public places. He even took part in conspiratorial meetings, which he naïvely imagined were unknown to the authorities. In the spring of 1938, for example, when I was with him in Milan to arrange programs for the fall and winter broadcasts in America, I was surprised to see him leave his house promptly at eleven on certain mornings. I thought he might be going for a walk, and I offered to accompany him. But he said: "No," and looked very mysterious. Later he confessed that he was a member of a group of elderly anti-Fascists who met secretly (as they thought) in the rear room of a small bookshop owned by one of them. As all of Toscanini's movements were closely watched by the police, the Fascists either discounted the seriousness of the little conspiracy or else were under orders from Mussolini not to interfere with him. At any rate, the bookshop was never raided, and the Maestro enjoyed the belief that he was outwitting the secret police.

Many of his old friends and associates avoided him through fear of being branded anti-Fascist by association; but the Italian people did not hesitate to show their love and admiration for him. He had nothing but contempt for his fair-weather friends, but he disapproved also of public demonstrations in his favor, which he took to be political rather than personal. He honestly thought of himself as a non-political person, and he saw no inconsistency in his public and private attacks on Mussolini and the regime.

One rainy night in Milan he accompanied me to the Conservatorio to hear the debut of a French violinist. His car deposited us at the conservatory hall, and Emilio, the chauffeur, was told to come back for us at the close of the concert. As we entered the hall the audience rose in a

body and shouted: *"Viva* Toscanini!" The Maestro
turned pale with anger and rushed out of the hall. I followed, of course, and so did half of the audience. In the
roofless courtyard of the building the Maestro raged
against the *"villani"* who failed to respect his privacy and
used him "politically." He then implored me to return
to the hall and let him go home alone. It was raining
hard, and he and I and the people who had formed a
ring around·us were being drenched. The car was nowhere in sight, and I said I would not hear of his going
home alone. But he clasped his hands close to my face
and, in a voice full of suffering, said: "I pray you, go
back. I am very unhappy. You must not fol-*low* me. You
must listen to the concert. I pray you . . . let me
go. . . ." There was nothing for me to do but obey. He
vanished in the darkness, and I and the curious who had
followed us into the courtyard returned to the hall.

His hatred of Mussolini was personal as well as political. At the end of World War I, Mussolini, then an
obscure Milanese journalist, had persuaded Toscanini to
be a candidate for some minor municipal office along
with him on a Socialist ticket. Mussolini's powers of persuasion must have been formidable indeed to overcome
Toscanini's distaste for politics. In addition, the country
had been beggared by defeat, and the situation of the
Italian worker and peasant was desperate; and it was un-
questionably Toscanini's concern for the lot of the un-
derdog that steered him into politics. In the elections
both Mussolini and Toscanini were snowed under.

Toscanini, much relieved, gladly resumed his baton. But Mussolini, not at all disheartened, set about creating the Fascist party and planning his march on Rome.

For years Toscanini had watched with growing hatred the transformation of the former liberal into a Fascist dictator. He now enlisted his reckless courage and his worldwide prestige in a personal war against the spurious Cæsar. From the time of Mussolini's march on Rome to his ignominious death, Toscanini was a thorn in his side. Mussolini could easily have had him put out of the way. In fact, it was rumored that Hitler had expressed surprise that his Italian counterpart tolerated this "senile and irritating musician." Such a man, he implied, would get short shrift in Germany. And the only explanation for Mussolini's sufferance may have been his fear of world opinion and his genuine admiration for a fellow dictator in a different realm, but one with greater personal courage in the pursuit of an ideal as selfless as his was selfish.

However, being unwilling to do away with Toscanini, Mussolini decided to woo him. Through intermediaries he made several advances for a meeting. These Toscanini scornfully rejected. Only once did he give way to pressure and reluctantly accede to a meeting with Il Duce; a committee representing the artists of La Scala had called on him to report on the desperate state of Italy's leading opera house. Il Duce had cut the government's usual subsidy of La Scala to an extent that seriously impaired the livelihood of even top-flight singers.

These were certain that the direct intervention of the Maestro would alter the situation. In fact, they had heard that the Duce was most eager to be reconciled with the Maestro, and they thought that even a formal call by Toscanini would materially improve the fortunes of La Scala. Mussolini happened to be in Milan at the moment. He had already been sounded out about a meeting with Toscanini, and was ready to receive him. The committee pleaded with the Maestro for hours before he yielded. An appointment was arranged, and at last, after many years, the Maestro found himself again in the presence of his former political running-mate.

In relating the incident the Maestro grew as pale as he said he had been when he stood before Mussolini. "I was wet through and through like after a rehearsal. I did not look in his face. He spoke a long time. I did not hear what he said. I did not reply. When I could not longer stand to be there, I turned around and left. It was a fiasco because I forget what I came to say. I wish-ed only to put my hands on his neck and choke him. Ah, *miseria!* It was wrong for me to be persuaded to come. I must always do only what I *feel* to do, not what I *think* to do."

In the late summer of 1938, presumably on Mussolini's orders, the police took away Toscanini's passport. Far from being dispirited, the Maestro was elated by this open reprisal. He was determined to get to America to carry out his commitment to NBC, and he conspired to have a seaplane take him from Lago Maggiore to a

Swiss lake, whence he could proceed unmolested to America. He entered with great zest into secret arrangements for this hazardous and perhaps fatal undertaking. The necessity for escape was, however, soon obviated. Whether because of the pressure brought to bear on Mussolini by Washington or through the intercession of influential Italians, the passport was restored in time for the Maestro to conduct his scheduled broadcast in New York in October. I believe the Maestro rather regretted the turn of events which enabled him to leave Milan by train. He would much have preferred a dangerous escape by plane in the dead of night.

Except for the situations created by his own unpredictable temperament, Toscanini's life in New York from 1939 to 1945 was ideal. In Riverdale, New York, overlooking the Hudson, he had bought a massive, roomy, late-Victorian house that had a central hall two stories high with an old-fashioned grand staircase leading to a balcony in the shape of a quandrangle. The Maestro was proud of the grand staircase, and would find many occasions to show it off by running up to his bedroom or sitting-room to fetch a letter, manuscript, or picture, disdaining all offers of servants or friends to run errands for him. "If I were not asham-ed for an old man, I would run up the stairs two at a time," he would say. Among his many endearing traits was his consideration for servants. I never noticed a hint of superiority in his behavior toward them. He addressed them as he did his family and friends. "Thank you, *caro*," he would say to one who opened the door for him, or "Do not trouble, my dear," and on arriving home after a long absence he might embrace the domestics warmly.

The Riverdale house was the scene of many entertainments and parties, at Christmas and New Year's and in the late spring, when the Maestro entertained the members of his orchestra and their wives. Always a hospitable host, he was never more solicitous for his guests than at his parties for his orchestra. He went about the tables urging everyone to eat and drink; he fascinated his guests with charming anecdotes. It was, in fact, impossible to believe that this benign, silver-haired old man was the same who perhaps only the day before at rehearsal had thundered at his men with the voice of an angry Jove, had broken his baton into bits, upset the heavy iron music stand at his side with a kick of his foot, and blundered off the stage in a blind Olympian rage. At those moments no object on his person or near him was safe from destruction. During a certain historic outburst, after he had deliberately ground a valuable watch to bits under his heel, Mr. Royal presented him with a brace of Ingersoll watches (then a dollar apiece) to break when necessity demanded it, thus saving from destruction a number of expensive timepieces the Maestro owned. Far from being affronted by so pointed a gift, Toscanini appreciated the serious intention of the donor. In due time the Ingersolls disappeared under the Maestro's annihilating heel.

Occasionally the orchestra and the Maestro gave a

live concert in cities not too far from New York. These trips brought with them special hazards and problems. At NBC we had worked out a system that ensured privacy for Toscanini. But away from our offices at 30 Rockefeller Plaza we were faced with such obstacles as the dubious acoustics of concert halls and the persistence of admirers of Toscanini in getting to see him at close range. The flavor of these expeditions out of New York may be sensed in the following typewritten report of a trip to near-by Newark. The writer was Albert Walker, an NBC employee assigned to look after the Maestro. Until he met Toscanini, Walker knew nothing of music; but, speedily falling a victim to the Maestro's charm, he soon began to hum snatches of Beethoven and Brahms as he briskly went about his duties of keeping strangers away from the Maestro and tending to his personal wants.

Toscanini Concert
Newark, N.J.

At 3:16 p.m. Tuesday, December 13th, we left the Astor. (Route taken to Holland Tunnel—West on 45th Street, South on the Westside Highway to Canal Street, through tunnel to New Jersey. Left tunnel at 3:31 p.m., picked up by pre-arranged police escort; after a wild ride—12 miles—arrived at Hotel Essex at 3:42 p.m.—average per hour, 60 miles.)

Maestro asked to drive around Newark; took advantage of this to locate the RR Terminal that Walter Toscanini was to arrive at.

Back to Mosque Theatre for rehearsal 4:30 p.m. Everything went great until 5:45. I was busy with details out front of theatre and Mrs. T. discovered that she forgot the Maestro's suspenders. So she sent the chauffeur to the hotel for same. The chauffeur came back at 6:00, and as he jumped out of the car, shut the car door, the damned thing locked on him. (He did not know this at the moment.) At 6:15 I went downstairs to check on flashlight hounds and told the chauffeur I would bring the Maestro down. I tried the door and imagine my feelings when we discovered the car locked. Not wanting to tell and upset the Maestro, I suggested that we go out front and see the theatre. He fell for it, so simply walked around the foyer and out to the street. Once there, we just walked back to the hotel (6:20). In the meantime we got the door opened!

Up to the Maestro's room and Mrs. T. told me to meet Walter at depot at 7:01. So I took time off for dinner and asked the chauffeur to pick me up at 6:50. Down to the Penn Station, and there was no train due at 7:01. Shot over to the Central of N.J. and no train due at 7:01. So back to Penn RR and found a 7:31. Waited for that one and Walter was aboard. Delivered him okay at 7:45. Went up to my room and hell broke out on my phone. A swarm of press and photographers were in the lobby. They all wanted pictures and were bound to get them. After telling them about the flash and arguing with them, I got a call that the Maestro was going to start for the theatre in about 25 minutes. So I dashed for my room and started to change for concert (time, 8: 10 p.m.). Mrs. T. called me and told me they were ready and would send the Maestro's bag to my room. Then I heard a noise outside of my door and opened to behold at least five photo men there. I argued with them and pleaded not to snap the Maestro when he came out. They got peeved and said they would. So I called the Hotel manager to clear the corridor. I made a bargain with the press men, if they saw us in the lobby, okay to shoot. I got dressed at last and called a war conference. The plan was to have Walter T. get off at the lobby and stand there and say out loud that he wished the Maestro would hurry. In the meantime I took the Maestro down in the elevator, putting out the lights and disconnecting the elevator indicator (so the press did not know where we got on or off). We got out through the basement and walked out the alley to the car. Reached the theatre at 8: 25 and, holy smokes, the bellhop took the wrong bag to the car! I beat it back to the hotel, up to the room and tried to unlock the door. The g–d— door would not open as the inside lock was down; did not have time to get master key; looked around for a fire axe and wedged it into the panel, pried it open and unlocked the door and rushed to the theatre, and as I flopped in the Maestro was just going out. The country was saved and I was K.O.'d after running four city blocks with the bag!

Going out of the theatre we had no trouble, as I had the car pulled right into the alley, dispossessing the fire chief's car, and the Maestro simply opened the stage door and into his car. A nice leisurely ride to New York and so to bed about 2:45 a.m.

Albert Walker

The presence of the Maestro offered perpetual excitement for us at NBC. As general musical director of NBC, I was often away from the symphony rehearsals, but in my office I received frequent bulletins by telephone about the condition of the Maestro's uneven disposition. These phone calls sounded like the weather reports of a Channel crossing: "all calm," "blue skies," "sun out," or else "rough sea," "fair to middling," "squalls," or "storm any minute." These messages often sent me hurrying to 8H. Sometimes a squall would have turned into blue skies by the time I got there. At other times I would find the storm raging in full force. My presence had, of course, no effect on the progress of the Maestro's ill-humor. But if, as often happened, he angrily terminated the rehearsal and retired to sulk and rage in his room, I would surreptitiously countermand his order to the men and, by applying a psychological treatment that long experience had perfected, would sometimes mollify him and persuade him to proceed with the rehearsal.

The method I used was simple indeed; it was based on the notorious singlemindedness of geniuses, and consisted of violently diversionary suggestions. I could divert his rage at his orchestra to something quite unrelated, which in turn made him forget the original cause of his unhappiness. For example, I would wait for a pause in his denunciation of his men and remark innocently: "I see the critics are raving about the beautiful tone of the ⸺ Orchestra." The Maestro would look up sharply and explode: "Don't speak to me about critics! They know no-*thing!* They think because the violins vibrate all the time—" the Maestro would put his left hand on his heart and do an imaginary slow vibrato with his middle finger —"they make a beautiful tone! No! A *fast* vibrato make a beautiful tone, not a slow one. Our NBC violins make quick vibrato. *That* make a beautiful tone." And he would embark on the virtues of his own orchestra, which he had a moment earlier consigned to perdition. While he was talking I would hold up his rehearsal coat, and through force of habit he would slip his arms through it. A few moments later he would follow me docilely into 8H, where the men, already alerted, sat in nervous silence. It was plain that the Maestro had completely forgotten the alleged sins of his own orchestra and was brooding now on the insensitiveness of music critics. The rehearsal was resumed and bade fair to continue without incident. I would go back to my office and await further bulletins.

The excitement, however, was not always induced by his surpassing art. Because NBC is a business operated for profit and accountable to stockholders, Toscanini's demands sometimes—indeed, quite often—interfered with the operations of the commercial programs, the profits from which paid for Toscanini and the NBC Symphony Orchestra.

The orchestra, for example, was assigned to play commercial programs when free from its symphonic duties. And as seventy-five or eighty per cent of its playing-time was given over to the rehearsals and broadcasts of the Symphony, its commercial programs were necessarily few. It happened one winter that Toscanini was rehearsing with the NBC Symphony in Carnegie Hall for a benefit concert that he was unselfishly donating to some worthy charity. The Maestro and the orchestra had been scheduled for the usual two-and-one-half-hour rehearsal from 4:00 to 6:30 p.m. on a certain day. At 8:00 p.m. thirty members of the orchestra were scheduled to play a commercial radio program at the NBC Studios, seven blocks south of Carnegie Hall. The Maestro sometimes ran over his allotted time at rehearsals, and I felt that a one-and-one-half-hour lapse between the end of his rehearsal and the NBC commercial program was more than sufficient leeway.

But at 6:30 the Maestro showed no disposition to finish. Nor at 7:00 or 7:15. The composition was Verdi's

Requiem, and for three and one-half hours the Maestro lavished his interpretative genius on the music and inspired his men to feats of lyric and dramatic expression which Carnegie Hall had seldom witnessed. Yet the eight-o'clock commercial program *had* to be serviced. The Maestro, of course, knew nothing about the *"com-mer-ziale,"* and would have cared less for anything so mundane, had he known. The orchestra contractor, whose duty it was to see that the thirty men were in their places at NBC in time to play the commercial, had been in a dreadful state for the last hour, frequently coming to me anxiously for instructions. "He must finish any moment," I kept telling him. But now it was 7:30, and we could no longer wait. I looked at the Maestro. He was in a fury of movement, shouting, pleading, singing, and dedicating all of his faculties to the molding of the great threnody. He could no more be stopped than an express train going at a fantastic speed. There seemed only one thing to do. I told the contractor to go down to the rim of the stage and from behind Toscanini beckon the needed players to leave one at a time and at spaced intervals. I had a faint hope that this defection of the men might go unnoticed by the nearsighted, galvanized Maestro. One by one the needed men stopped playing, crouched low, and sneaked off the stage as inconspicuously as they could manage. For a long time the Maestro did not notice the maneuver. Then suddenly, in a pause in the music, he became aware of empty chairs in strategic sections of the orchestra and

109

caught a man doubled up in the very act of leaving his place. With a cry of rage, the Maestro wheeled around and shouted my name. But my nerves were already too shaken for me to face his wrath. I ran from the hall ignominiously, jumped into a cab, was driven home, gained my room, and fell exhausted on the bed. I heard later that the Maestro, finding me gone, tore his collar to shreds, upset every inanimate object that stood in his way, ground his Ingersoll to bits, staggered blindly off the stage and into his dressing-room. However, he was bent on going through with the benefit, and as he never permitted anything, not even his rages, to stop him from doing what he wanted to do, the concert took place. But the next day, taking advantage of one of his calmer moments, I was able to dramatize the need of the *"commerziale"* program for the thirty men who had been spirited away. Any crisis was sure to enlist his sympathy. His mood changed overnight, and all was well again.

During the war years he suffered periods of acute depression, which were reflected in his behavior at rehearsals. He would arrive at the studio silent and scowling, and after a few minutes of rehearsal get into a rage and dismiss the orchestra. It transpired that the Maestro had heard over the radio that morning a report of an Allied setback, in consequence of which he had not touched his breakfast and had talked of conducting as a futile waving of one's arms while civilization was going down the drain.

But he could never long resist the power of music,

which consciously and unconsciously filled his waking hours. I remember the faraway, dreamlike, spiritual ecstasy expressed in his face and body after a rehearsal of Wagner's *Siegfried Idyll*. He had stepped off the podium, dripping as usual from head to foot, and had walked into his room. I attempted to divest him of his jacket and shirt, but he stood immovable as in a trance, his hands clasped, eyes shut and freshets of perspiration raining down from his head and eyebrows. I wiped his head and face with a towel, but he did not move. At last I said: "You must change into dry clothes or you will catch cold." He held out his arms dutifully and I began to remove his jacket. Suddenly he interrupted my efforts by clasping his hands again. "It is more than fifty years since I first conduct this music," he said quietly, as if talking to himself, "yet every time is like the first time for me. I cannot bear it—it is too beautiful. Think! Ima*gine* how Cosima felt on that morning when she was awake-en-ed by the sound of the *Idyll!*" And he again stood motionless for some moments as he gave himself up to the contemplation of that memorable scene at the villa on Lake Lucerne when, on the staircase leading to his wife's bedroom, Wagner conducted a little orchestra of eleven men in the piece he had composed to celebrate the birth of his son Siegfried.

The spell that Toscanini cast on everyone around him during those years was powerful and unflagging. Whether grave or gay, vengeful or beneficent, he magnetized alike players, page boys, servants, executives, friends, and even his family. They trembled at his frown and basked in his smile. At NBC his every wish was attended to in the spirit of a favor conferred by him. To be allowed to remove his sopping garments was like assisting at a rite. To sit next to him in a motor car or at table, to have him address one as *"caro,"* to attend a concert or a play with him, to entertain him—all these became memorable events. No one stopped to examine and analyze or question his strange and unprecedented power. He ruled over our hearts and minds. His judgments were accepted like articles of faith. We took to our hearts the people he liked and looked askance at those he dropped. We loved the music he loved, became skeptical about the music he despised, and accepted without question the music that, having summarily cast out, he as summarily restored to favor. When with him we talked about him. We never tired of hearing him talk about himself; when away from him we never ceased recalling his words, looks, gestures, opinions. When he telephoned to one of us, we hastily apprised one another, through a telephone relay, of the happy occurrence. And indeed it was thrilling to lift up the receiver and hear one's name pronounced *sotto voce*, hoarsely, vibrating with the fast tremolo so characteristic of the Maestro's speech.

We spent much of our leisure time in thinking up ways to amuse him. At the end of one season we planned to surprise him with a great party at the Sarnoffs', which was to be in the form of an old-fashioned vaudeville show put on and performed by his friends. The enterprise was of considerable magnitude, and brought with it great anxieties, for the participants were amateurs like myself, and the professionals among us assumed roles quite outside their specialties. Marc Connelly, the playwright, staged the show and acted in one of the sketches; Walter Toscanini, the Maestro's son, danced a Russian Hopak, while Efrem Zimbalist, in Russian peasant costume, played the harmonica. An acrobatic number enlisted the clumsy gymnastics of six amateurs, all dressed in tights and spangles; while I, in white tie and tails that swept the floor, sang Victor Herbert's "Ah, Sweet Mystery of Life" and led the grand finale. Rehearsals went on for weeks, and a professional tumbler was hired to coach the gymnasts in their routine.

All this was kept secret from the Maestro. On the day of the show Mrs. Toscanini told him only that they were to dine that evening at the Sarnoffs'. When they arrived at the house, they found themselves in a press of people all in evening dress. The raucous noise of a jazz band smote the Maestro's ears. He thought they had mistaken the house. But his wife assured him they hadn't, and piloted him into a great solarium on the top floor, which had been fitted up to look like a Broadway night club, with small tables, a dance floor, and a thick velvet rope barring the entrance. At the rope stood Mr. Royal, dressed as a headwaiter and made unrecognizable by a strange wig. He consulted a sheet of paper in his hand, asked the by-now-bewildered Maestro his name, and, on being told, commanded him to spell it. This the Maestro did, and the "headwaiter," glancing up and down his paper, said that no reservation had been made in any such name. The Maestro, utterly at a loss, was about to turn tail when Mr. Royal, fearing the joke had gone too far, removed the rope, passed them through, and showed them to a table in the very first row. The Maestro glared about him, sat down, dropped his head on his chest, covered his eyes with his hand, and remained so for the rest of the evening. The guests, about eighty in number, surrounded him, but the Maestro's ostentatious unhappiness put a damper on everybody, and more particularly on the cast, who were appalled at the prospect of displaying their amateur talents before the grim, unseeing, hostile guest of honor. Some of the actors, having taken a peep at the Maestro through the wings, burst into tears and vowed not to go on. But the feelings of the other guests had to be considered, and at a hurried meeting of the cast backstage it was decided to proceed with the show. So the show went on, unseen by the Maestro, and only nervously observed by the guests, whose attention shifted alternately from the stage to the brooding conductor. The injustice and the unfairness of the Maestro's behavior had their effect on those who had worked so hard to amuse him. A certain bravado now animated the cast as it went through its paces. The acrobats leaped higher than they had at rehearsals. Walter Toscanini executed his Russian dance with a gusto that subsequently laid him up with an injured leg for weeks; Marcia

Davenport, attempting a split during a can-can number, landed on the floor with such force as to be obliged to wear a cast for her injured back for months; and I, with the aid of a concealed microphone in the lapel of my tailcoat, advanced boldly to the Toscanini table and roared "Ah, Sweet Mystery of Life" straight into the Maestro's frozen face.

There was supper and dancing after the show. Still the Maestro sat unmoving, his hand over his eyes. Fair ladies came and sat beside him and attempted to flirt. Mrs. Sarnoff brought him food especially cooked to his taste. It was all to no avail. Mrs. Toscanini, apologetic and embarrassed, attempted to explain that her husband had been upset by the noise and the lights, and that he did not like surprises on principle. At one in the morning, with tears in her eyes, she begged her husband to go home. "I will stay to the bitter end," he muttered gloomily, in the voice of one condemned. So he stayed on, prolonging the pall he had cast over the party, while the jazz orchestra blared away and the people ate and danced halfheartedly and finally melted away. Mr. and Mrs. Toscanini were among the last to go, leaving the indignant cast to express their resentment openly and take what comfort they might in recalling the polite expressions of sympathy from the rest of the audience.

This unfortunate episode had, however, a pleasant sequel. For, having indulged his spleen to the full, the Maestro began to regret the pain he had caused. Some time later he conveyed his repentance obliquely by suggesting that if we ever gave another show, he would like to be a participant. This unexpected offer instantly obliterated whatever resentment we still felt. We hastily made plans for another show with the Maestro as star. We concocted a series of comedy turns and sketches, and recruited a cast of celebrated artists. The presence of Toscanini and a half-dozen popular soloists gave us an excuse for presenting the entertainment as a benefit for the Chatham Square Music School, a non-profit school for talented young musicians on New York's lower East Side. Even so, we failed to grasp fully the drawing-power of a cast that included Toscanini, Heifetz, Horowitz, Tibbett, Milstein, Adolph Busch, Alfred Wallenstein, and the late Emanuel Feuermann.

Although we could have sold out Madison Square Garden, we rented the tiny Chanin Theater, seating two hundred persons. We had printed and mailed out invitations to purchase tickets at fifteen dollars apiece, but the price also included a midnight supper and dance with liquor and food. For a time our ticket sale was negligible. On investigation we learned that most of those to whom we mailed invitations refused to believe that the cast of characters for a revue entitled *Say Ah!* could possibly include some of the greatest musical artists in the world. Believing themselves the victims of a hoax, they had thrown the invitations into their wastepaper baskets. But two or three days before the night of the performance, word got around that Toscanini, Heifetz, Horowitz, Feuermann, *et al*, were actually rehearsing for *Say Ah!* We sold all the tickets in one afternoon, disappointing many persons who telephoned too late.

The Maestro's "number" in *Say Ah!* was called "Toscanini and his Children's Orchestra." It was a take-off on a "Youth Orchestra" then recently organized by Leopold Stokowski. The Maestro's "Children's Orchestra" consisted of some thirty instrumentalists, with Heifetz as concertmaster. They were to appear in short pants and white blouses, and the Maestro was to wear a long, old-fashioned Prince Albert coat, with a bandanna handkerchief sticking out of a rear pocket, an exaggerated starched collar, and a large four-in-hand. The music he selected included short popular pieces such as "*Loin du Bal,*" "Tritsch-tratsch Polka," "Skaters' Waltz," and Mozart's farcical "A Musical Joke."

A dress rehearsal was called for very late in the evening of the night before the performance. Out of deference to the Maestro, we asked him to rehearse his number first, though it came last on the program. This mark of respect almost resulted in the abandonment of the show. For the Maestro rehearsed his little pieces as painstakingly and arduously as if they had been exalted works of Beethoven. If the members of the orchestra had thoughts of enjoying themselves in the preparation of light "hotel" music like "*Loin du Bal,*" they were quickly disabused. For three hours Toscanini and the little band of noted instrumentalists labored to perfect the small pieces until they sounded like miracles of orchestral balance. As we of the non-musical cast listened, we were

117

struck by the inferior quality of our own poor amateur dramatic efforts. Some of us flatly announced that we would withdraw. Mr. Herbert Graf, our stage director, observed sadly that we could not possibly appear on a program with Toscanini and his remarkable players, and he suggested that the Maestro enlarge his portion of the program to a full evening's entertainment. We all agreed, with the exception of one amateur dancer who was to have been the star in a burlesque of a ballet to the music of Debussy's "Afternoon of a Faun." Made unhappy by the decision to abandon everything in the show but the Toscanini "number," this fledgling Nijinsky fled to a dressing-room, where I discovered him lying on the floor dressed in his faun's costume, alternately sobbing and drinking from a bottle of whisky he had thoughtfully provided for himself.

I informed the Maestro of our decision as he took his place in the first row of the theater to watch the re-hearsal of the rest of the show. He expressed great sur-prise, but declared that he would reserve judgment until he had an opportunity to see for himself. By then it was one a.m. I hurriedly rounded up the actors. Nervous and shaken, we went through our numbers while the Maestro watched us intently through his pince-nez, which he held lengthwise in front of him. After the final number I leaned over the stage and with sinking heart asked him what he thought. "Wonderful!" he said gravely. I brought the glad news to my dejected and perspiring colleagues, and we spent several hours celebrating.

The next evening I arrived early at the theater. Only the Maestro was backstage, dressed in the Prince Albert (he had spent half a day at Brooks Brothers being fitted) and nervously pacing up and down. Soon the rest of the cast arrived and were crowded into the few little dressing-rooms the tiny theater afforded. Half-dressed actors kept rushing in and out of the corridor, jostling the Maestro, who, having dressed at home, did not rate a dressing-room. He got in everybody's way, but there was no place else for him to go. As his was the last number on the program, he would have been in ample time had he arrived at ten instead of seven. When reminded of this, he said it was his habit to arrive at a performance ahead of the audience.

The show was a stunning success. A sketch in which Heifetz (as a barefoot, tatterdemalion Tennessee hillbilly), Horowitz (as a Dostoyevsky-ish piano student), Tibbett (as a vainglorious singer), and Feuermann (as a Tyrolese cellist) applied for admission to the Chatham Square Music School brought down the house. Heifetz played a Virginia reel on an inexpensive violin, which I, in the character of the school's director, broke irately over his head. Horowitz, looking like a character out of Gorky's *The Lower Depths*, kept mumbling idiotically: "I play the piano" when asked what he would play. Mr. Tibbett, clad in white tie and tails, came out to sing the Prologue from *Pagliacci*, which he did seriously and beautifully. But at a certain point his trousers began almost imperceptibly to slip down. At the final high G, delivered with clarion force and tonal beauty, they fell to the floor as the stage quickly blacked out. The house rocked with laughter. Rachmaninoff, sitting in the balcony, seemed to resent the planned accident at the Prologue's climax, and he left the theater, presumably in displeasure.

Another sketch warmly greeted was "The Maestro Comes to Dinner," which spoofed the terror inspired by the Maestro's acceptance of a dinner engagement. Wanda Horowitz, Toscanini's daughter, assumed the role of her father and looked startlingly like him in get-up and bearing—so much so that many in the audience thought that the Maestro was playing himself. In the skit the hostess discovers, a moment before the arrival of her distinguished guest, that the cook has put too much salt in the *polenta*. Unwilling to face the Maestro's wrath, the family decides to commit suicide in a body. The host draws a revolver and shoots everyone in the room. Each one dies resignedly. But Mrs. Heifetz, the mother of the violinist, injected an impromptu line as she expired: "Good-by, Jascha," she gasped, "I know *you* will understand!"

The climax of the evening came at the end with Toscanini and his Children's Orchestra. Never had light music been played with such brilliance, verve, beauty, tonal balance, and general perfection! In a certain crescendo-decrescendo passage in Mozart's "A Musical Joke," Toscanini made the men of the orchestra rise slowly to their feet and then sink slowly back. The audience stood up and cheered. And the Maestro, loath, as usual, to take curtain calls alone, made his "children" rise innumerable times as he stepped down from the podium and took his place among them. After the show, artists and audience repaired to a large adjoining room for supper and dancing to the music of a jazz band. Our joy at the success of the show was slightly tempered with regret that the Chatham Square School benefited only to the extent of $2,200 instead of the great sum the presence of such stars should have netted.

CHAPTER SIX

$\mathscr{I}$N the spring of 1940 Toscanini and the NBC Symphony sailed on a tour of South America. The Maestro had a pleasant time on the boat. Each morning he appeared on deck dressed in colorful silk pajamas. He talked at great length to the men in the orchestra, and he was generally surrounded by many of them eagerly taking in his every word, while those who had cameras hovered at a distance and snapped the Maestro, catching him in characteristic attitudes. He watched with great interest the activities of his musicians, the shuffleboard contests and swimming in the pool, the noisy rites celebrating the crossing of the equator. One member of our party, a quiet, middle-aged man with a family to support, fell a victim to the lure of a coin machine in the lounge, losing more than he was able to afford. Neither his colleagues nor I could detach him from the machine. In desperation I appealed to the Maestro, who said he would speak to the man. We watched the Maestro enter the salon and go up to the man, who was completely absorbed in feeding quarter after quarter into the insatiable contraption. However, the reprimand that Toscanini had prepared was never delivered. For the Maestro himself became fascinated by the machine, and half an hour later he was still standing at the side of the player, and with him patiently waiting for the elusive jackpot to come tumbling out of the slot. "I said something to him, but he did not listen," he explained rather apologetically later. "You know, I like-ed that machine."

Never before had the men of the orchestra been so close to their adored Maestro, and never before had my wife and I been privileged to see so much of him for so long a time. Except during the five or so hours between four and nine in the morning when he went down to his suite, presumably to rest and sleep, we were with him every moment of the day and night. Mrs. Toscanini would most sensibly retire at a normal hour. Not so the Maestro. He would watch the dancing in the salon until the band and the dancers dispersed in the early dawn. He would then announce that he felt not at all sleepy and meant to walk the deck and look at the sea and sky. We could not, of course—nor did we really ever wish to —leave him to himself. So, protesting that we too were not sleepy (though we might be dying on our feet), we walked on either side of him, back and forth the length of the deck, sometimes until we saw the top of the sun rising out of the sea. Then the Maestro, sensing but not understanding our exhaustion, would say: "Go to bed, you are tired. I? No! But I will go to my room."

One morning the Maestro heard on the short-wave radio that France had capitulated to the Nazis. The news almost robbed him of his senses. He shut himself up in his rooms and for two days refused food and drink; and his voice, cursing and swearing at Hitler and Mussolini, was so loud that it penetrated to the deck above. At last, in the faint hope that I could calm him down or at least divert his rage toward some topic less world-shaking, I went into his room. He was walking up and down, screaming and shouting. I sat in a chair and waited for a chance to speak to him. It never came. With inexhaustible lung power he attacked, in Italian and English, the enemy, the allies and their leaders, and the entire human race. All at once the shadowy figure of his wife stood in the doorway of her bedroom, adjoining the little salon in which I sat. "*Basta! Basta!*" she yelled in a voice that cut through his, and he shut up as suddenly as if someone had placed a hand over his mouth. I sat frozen with apprehension; no one before had dared to raise a voice to him, let alone command him to be silent! Yet nothing happened. The Maestro looked at his wife wonderingly for a while. Then he slowly turned away, sank into a chair, put his hand over his eyes, and began swaying his head from left to right and right to left in the self-pitying manner I knew so well. Not another sound came from him. His wife retreated to her bedroom. I tiptoed out of the room, leaving the Maestro moaning softly to himself. Outside, I told the steward that the Maestro was now in a mood to eat something, and I asked him to bring him a cup of minestrone and some bread sticks.

The vacillating fortunes of the war were reflected in his behavior at home, at the houses of friends, and in his work. But his prophecy that he would one day "dance on the grave of Mussolini" was, in a figurative sense, borne out. One Sunday afternoon, in the intermission of one of Toscanini's broadcasts, the loudspeaker in Studio 8H suddenly announced the capture and execution of Mussolini. The Maestro, on the point of entering the hall to resume his concert, heard the name Mussolini, but could not understand the rest of the announcement. He turned to me in perplexity. His son, Walter, fearing that the shock would be too much for his father, motioned to me not to enlighten him. By coincidence, the program that afternoon was all-Italian, winding up with the Overture to Rossini's *William Tell*. This coincidence appeared to me providential, and I decided to risk telling the Maestro. He stood silent for an instant. Then he said quietly: *"Bene, bene . . .* now we must play well," and he walked briskly into the hall and onto the stage, to the shattering applause of an audience already excited by the news and wondering about its effect on the man who had prayed and hoped and worked for such a moment.

The end of the war brought a measure of serenity

125

to Toscanini and, by reflection, to the people who worked with him. The republic that succeeded the monarchy in Italy wished to honor him by conferring on him the title of Senator. The Maestro politely declined, as he had previously declined (with one exception) all offers of degrees from leading universities of America and England. "I am a moosician—not a doctor," he said. The presidents and trustees of universities were mystified by his refusals as something altogether beyond their experience with celebrated men. Oxford, in particular, was so pressing that Toscanini was touched. He wrote the trustees that, while he could not possibly accept a degree, he would be happy to give a concert for any benefit they would name. This he did in the little university town, raising an impressive number of pounds.

At NBC we had the recurring problem each year of persuading Toscanini that he was not too old to undertake another season of broadcasts. As early as 1941 he wrote to Mr. Sarnoff that he thought it was high time for him to withdraw from what he called the militant scene of art. He desired, of course, the reassurance of our faith in his artistic vigor and physical vitality, with which we duly besieged him. Almost every year of the seventeen he spent at NBC saw him formally (and in measured, archaic phrases) resigning his post and, following our heartfelt emotional pleas, permitting himself to reconsider. In the meantime he continued to make history in 8H and, later, in Carnegie Hall.

The younger generation of music-lovers had never

heard him conduct opera, and I used this fact as an argument to persuade the Maestro to broadcast concert performances of some noteworthy music dramas. In quick succession he prepared and directed *Fidelio, Orfeo, La Bohème, La Traviata, Aïda, Otello, Falstaff,* and *A Masked Ball.* All of these broadcasts, recorded on wax and, later, on tape, were subsequently released, or will be released, by RCA Victor. The rehearsals, with Toscanini at the piano and the singers grouped around him, offered to those fortunate enough to be present a glimpse of the working methods of a great musician and born stage director. For, while there could be no actual stage direction in a concert performance, Toscanini arrived at the same thing by inspiring the artists to give an illusion of dramatic action even more immediate than in a stage performance. And he could, in illustration, when criticism and suggestion failed, sing a phrase himself with his throaty, guttural voice in a manner that startlingly brought to the surface the dramatic or humorous point he wished to make.

The phrase *"Non so"* (I don't know) in Verdi's *Otello* drew from the Maestro a lecture to the baritone who was singing Iago; then, having failed to produce the result desired, the Maestro sang the two words in a manner that was altogether inimitable. "You see, *caro,*" Toscanini explained, "Iago is a bad man . . . but he is also clever . . . more clever than Otello, who is a child . . . far, far more clever . . . and when Otello ask to him why Cassio and Roderigo are fighting he answer

'*Non so!*' . . . But the way he say it must make Otello to think: 'Ah, he *does* know why, but he wishes not to get Cassio in trouble, he also wishes not to disturb me!' . . . At the same time he must make Otello suspect Cassio. . . . All these things Iago must convey with the words '*Non so.*' It is *difficile, caro . . . molto, molto.* . . . Perhaps it should sound like this . . ." And the Maestro sang "*Non so,*" and all the shrewdness and evil of Iago were in his voice and diction. At a rehearsal of *Traviata* the Maestro stopped playing, shook his head sadly, went to a bookcase, took down a copy of *Hamlet,* and read the entire "Speak the speech, I pray you" passage with great positiveness and many mispronunciations. "This," he commented, "is true for opera as well as for the stage. *Cari amici,* think to Shakespeare always!"

At the final rehearsals of *La Bohème* I undertook to give the signal for the offstage breaking of dishes in the third act. With the score before me, I watched for the composer's indication "Here a breaking of dishes is heard," and gave the signal to the sound-effects man who stood near me with a barrel of cheap crockery. At the crash I heard Toscanini screaming: "No! No!" and I put my head through the door and asked if anything had gone wrong. "Every*thing!*" the Maestro yelled. "Once more!" I returned to my post, the orchestra and singers began again, and again at the indicated place I nodded to the sound-effects man. The second crash again infuriated the Maestro. "Wrong! Wrong!" he screamed.

"What imbe*cile* is doing that?" Terrified, I had to confess that I was the one. "So it's you!" he stormed. "Don't you know you must wait to break dishes until the soprano and baritone finish their duet? . . . Imbe*cile* . . . Santa Maria . . . Santissima . . ." "But, Maestro," I said stoutly, "in the score Puccini says—" "Ah!" he broke in, "you do not use your brain. . . . *Si* . . . *certo* . . . Puccini say: 'Break dishes,' but he wishes the people first to hear the notes. No? He compose the notes to be *heard*, no? Imbe*cile!* Once more!" For the third try I used my brain and waited for Marcello and Musetta to finish their duet. The breakage this time was acceptable to the Maestro, for he made no comment.

The public performance of *La Bohème* was perfect until the final four bars of the opera. So great was the tension of the orchestra and the Maestro as the opera drew to a close that at the concluding chords the brasses entered a fraction of a second too soon. The error was so insignificant that only the nervous brasses and the Maestro could have noticed it. A moment later the opera was over and the audience broke into thunderous applause. The Maestro, with head bowed, left the stage and went swiftly to his dressing-room, leaving the singers to take their bows alone. Once in his room, the Maestro abandoned himself to an elemental rage more devastating than any I had ever witnessed. Screaming and roaring incomprehensible things, he tore at his clothing and upset every movable object that yielded to his inspired strength. His piano and a large desk resisted all his efforts at dislodgment, and in exasperation he kicked them repeatedly with such fury that I feared for his legs. After minutes of fulmination and wreakage he suddenly desisted and said: "Send me the *porci* [the swine]. I wish to speak with them." The erring players had not dared to leave the hall. There were nine of them, and I led them into the Maestro's room, where they took up an uneasy position in a line against a wall, their faces pale, their heads down. The Maestro walked up and down in front of them like a sergeant inspecting his squad, glaring at each one with hatred and contempt. At length he said with bitter sincerity: "I hide my head in shame. After what happen-ed tonight my life is fin-ish-ed. For me it is impossible to look in the face of any*bawdy*. *I* can live no more. But *you*—" and he pointed straight at the man at the head of the dejected line—"you will sleep with your wife tonight as if no*thing* happen-ed. I know you!" The Maestro turned away, and the men sadly filed out.

The telephone rang. It was my wife. She had ar-ranged a supper party for the Maestro and she won-dered what had delayed us. In cryptic monosyllables I managed to convey the state of affairs in the dressing-room. "Of course he won't come," she said. "I suppose it is just as well." I assured her that he would certainly go straight home. I would be home as soon as I had put him in his car and seen him off. As he slumped de-jectedly into the back seat of his car, I said: "Shall I tell the chauffeur to drive you home?" "No!" he answered bitterly, "to *your* house." I excused myself for a moment, ran back into the building, and telephoned my wife. "You better meet him at the door with a glass of champagne. He needs it. It may save your party."

My wife met us at the door with a glass of champagne in her hand. She kissed the Maestro and handed him the glass. "What is?" he said with an air of innocence which would have deceived anyone who did not know him intimately. "Champagne," said my wife. The Maestro shook his head. "Could you," he asked plaintively, "give me a glass of water? I would like some water." In our twenty years of friendship we had never seen the Maestro drink water. My wife and I exchanged glances. It was now clear to us that the Maestro was still nursing his grievance at the brasses and was determined to prolong his pain and make us share it. We brought him a glass of water. He drank it avidly, like one parched in the desert who suddenly comes upon a water hole. "Ah! Good!" he exclaimed. "Can I have some more?" He emptied two large glasses, and we went in to dinner. He refused all food with excessive politeness, spoke no words except "Thank you, *cara*, no!" and "Is there more water?" The dinner was a nightmare. When it was over, he went into the living-room, sat down by himself, and covered his eyes with his hand. The guests conversed in low tones. The evening was ruined. I was angry with him for his punishment of persons innocent of any musical misdeeds. And, fearing that my anger would impel me to rudeness, I deliberately steered clear of him. My aloofness became so marked as the evening wore on that my wife implored me to pay some attention to the guest of honor. This I refused to do. It was not until one in the morning that the Maestro rose to go. I handed him his hat without a word, and he left. Half an hour later a friend of the Toscaninis rang up. "What have you done to the Maestro?" she asked. "He telephoned me a moment ago and said he had never been so insulted in his life." "Who does he think he is," he had exclaimed scornfully, "to treat a guest in his house with such rudeness? Where was he brought up? Was he never taught manners?" and so forth, and so forth.

There was to be a rehearsal next morning. Assuming that the Maestro would never speak to me again, I asked the lady whether she thought I had better stay away. She said she would speak to the Maestro and call me back. At two in the morning she called. The Maestro was still very angry, but wasn't it my duty to be at rehearsals? he had asked. Next morning, a few minutes before the time of rehearsal, I opened the door of his dressing-room. He was sitting at the piano playing softly the prelude to the last act of Catalani's opera *La Wally*, and pretending not to see me. He looked beautifully serene, and the expression on his face was angelic. I was completely unnerved by his appearance. A feeling of guilt smote me. I went behind him and listened to his playing awhile. Then I succumbed to an expiatory impulse and put my arms around him. He stopped playing, turned around, and embraced me. "What beautiful music!" he said. "How simple and noble. The snow is falling softly, sadly . . ."

In the intermission, after he had rehearsed Beethoven's Eighth Symphony, the Maestro startled me with a question. "What would you think, *caro*," he asked, "if I reinforced the orchestration of the theme in the first movement when it arrives *fff*. You know, I have not slept nights thinking to it. It is very seldom that Beethoven puts three fortes; that means he wants the theme to sound very strong. But what happens? It does not sound strong. Perhaps in Beethoven's mind it sounded strong. But he was deaf, and he never heard it played. Do you think I dare change? I would like to add tympani and brasses. Then it would sound *fff* the way Beethoven really wished it to sound. Tell me frankly, *caro*. Do you think I dare?"

I replied that he was a better judge of such matters than I. We sat silent for some time. "I think to try," he finally said. The next morning he brought with him new parts for the percussion and brasses he had written out. I went into the auditorium to hear the new version of the passage. The Maestro played through the entire first movement. When the controversial passage arrived, it sounded distinctly different from the original. At the finish the Maestro faced the auditorium and called my name in a loud voice. I knew that he was going to ask me what I thought. But my opinion was unfavorable, and I decided not to reveal my presence. I slid under my seat. The Maestro waited awhile and then called my name in a louder voice. Several people around me who knew me began to look at me wonderingly. Realizing that my attempt at deception had failed, I rose and reluctantly made my way to the stage. When I stood below him, the Maestro said: "Have you heard?" I said I had. "What did you think?" I gulped and said weakly: "I didn't like it." I had the impression that everybody—the people out front and the orchestra on the stage—was frozen with horror at my temerity. The Maestro looked down on me remorselessly and said: "Why didn't you like?" I thrashed around in my mind for a reason, and surprised myself and horrified everyone else by saying: "I thought it was vulgar." A fearful silence filled the hall, as if everybody had stopped breathing. There was a long pause. The Maestro then said: "You are *syou-er* you heard?" I nodded. "I will now play the movement in the original, and after that once again with the new orchestration. Stay here and listen." The Maestro turned toward the orchestra. When he had finished both versions, he veered round to me again. I remained silent. "You still don't like?" he asked. "I don't like," I said. "Dolin," the Maestro called to the librarian, "take away what I have written." Nothing more was ever heard about the new version.

He welcomed criticism from any reliable quarter. "You know, I am so close to the orchestra I cannot hear many things." After rehearsals he would ask me whether I heard this or that, whether the "*balance*" had been good, and so forth, and he listened to what I (or anyone

else who took him at his word) had to say with the de-
tachment of one who is interested only in the end result. When he played contemporary music, he insisted
on the continual presence of the composer, whom he
consulted frequently. Once, at a rehearsal of a modern
work, I was enraged at the many interruptions by the
composer, a brash and insensitive young man who
stopped the Maestro every few minutes to tell him how
he wanted his composition played. He even gesticulated
to the players from behind the Maestro's back. When I
complained about the behavior of this individual, the
Maestro regarded me with wonder. "But he is the *composer*," he said reprovingly. "*He* knows better than I
how his music should sound."

When the war ended, the Maestro began spending
his summers in Italy. La Scala had been badly damaged
by Allied bombs, and he took a direct interest in the
restoration of the theater. When it was its old self again
—except for the wonderful acoustics, which, the Maestro maintained, unaccountably resisted restoration—he
opened it with a great concert for the benefit of the orchestra. The following spring he conducted at La Scala
acts from Boïto's *Nerone* and *Mefistofele*. This he did
by way of atoning for his fancied (or perhaps real) neg-
lect of Boïto at the time of the composer's last illness
and death. Boïto had been his great friend and, in a
sense, his mentor and sponsor. "You must hear Toscanini conduct your *Falstaff*," Boïto had once said to

Verdi. "You would be content." Verdi, alas, never heard Toscanini conduct. The preparations for the excerpts from Boïto's two operas turned Toscanini's apartment in the Via Durini into rehearsal rooms. People from La Scala came and went continually; singers were coached, there were sessions with the chorus master, with the scenic designer and the stage director, Toscanini attending to the smallest details of the production. Great outbursts of temper, musical corrections in a raucous voice, and threats of abandonment of the project were followed by expressions of satisfaction and pleasure and a personal show of cordial hospitality, when *"espresso"* and Carpano were brought in and the artists relaxed under the Maestro's paternal smile.

Mrs. Toscanini was generally confined to her room —their room, for the Maestro had no bedroom of his own—with the illness that was soon to prove fatal. She had stayed in Milan under care of her doctor during the winter while her husband was conducting in New York, and when he arrived at the Via Durini she was scarcely able to get up from her bed to greet him. In preparation for his coming she had engaged a special chef, who came by the day, and who could be glimpsed through the open kitchen door in his white jacket and tall chef's hat and, after dinner, in ordinary clothes, passing through the dining-room on his way out, carrying his own culinary tools in a satchel, bowing elaborately and saying: *"Buona notte, Maestro."* To which the Maestro, not recognizing the man in his street clothes, would answer affably:

"*Ciao, caro,*" and look to his wife for enlightenment as to the man's identity.

I had accompanied Toscanini to Italy, and was invited to take my meals at his house. On the day of our arrival Mrs. Toscanini made a valiant effort to sit at table with us. The dining-table was a high one, and the chair his wife had designated for the Maestro was extremely low. Sitting down, he found to his surprise that the table was too high for comfort. But out of solicitude for his ailing wife he said nothing, and all that summer he ate his meals from an inconvenient elevation. His tenderness toward his wife was unfailing. Often at table he would reach out and place his hand over hers and gaze at her with great compassion. And knowing that she would be displeased if he ate sparingly, as he ordinarily did, he made a show of tasting the food elaborately prepared by the expensive chef; and he refrained, when guests were present, from calling attention, as was his wont, to his own abstemiousness. But once, after the departure of a luncheon guest who had eaten well, he forgot himself and said sarcastically: "From the way she ate, you would never believe that she had lost a son in the war!"

The gravity of his wife's condition preyed upon his mind at those scarce moments when he was not immersed in music. He had always taken for granted that he would survive his wife, who was ten years his junior. In the years when she was quite well he would say, apropos of the, to him, pernicious tendency of widowers

to remarry: "When Carla dies I will not marry again."
But as her illness progressed he began to brood over the
separation that would eventually face him, and he often
gave way to tears and wondered aloud whether he could
live without her.

When the end was approaching, he had just finished his season with the NBC Symphony in New York.
A cable arrived from Milan with the dreaded news, and
the Maestro flew at once to Italy. I saw him off at the
airport. He looked haggard and old. He moved slowly
and feebly, and there was an air of hopelessness about
him which was the more heartbreaking because I had
never before seen him surrender so completely to apathy
and almost childish self-pity. I did what I could to console him, pretending that her case was less grave than
we both knew it to be. I spoke about his return in the
fall and our plans for the season, and I mentioned his
pet project—a concert performance of Verdi's *A Masked
Ball*. He shook his head sadly, and tears ran down his
face. "No, *caro*," he moaned, "it is the end, my life is
finish-*ed* . . . finish-*ed*. . . ." He leaned on my arm
heavily as I walked him to the plane. Still weeping, he
bade me farewell. "*Addio, caro*," he whispered, "I pray
you to engage for *Un Ballo* [*A Masked Ball*] Bjoerling
[the tenor]. I pray you . . ." He ascended the steps of
the gangplank, and a moment later the plane was in the
air. Music had triumphed over life and death. I remembered and now understood his astonishing retort to an
Italian heart specialist who had pronounced the Mae-

stro's heart in beautiful condition—in fact, quite un-touched. "Why shouldn't it be?" the Maestro had said. "It has *never been used.*"

Nevertheless, after his wife's funeral he shut himself up in his gloomy apartment in Milan during one of the hottest summers on record, eating hardly enough to keep alive, listening to no music, and refusing to touch his piano or open a score, weeping bitterly over his loss and protesting that his life was over and that he wished only for death. It was at that time that I went to Italy, hoping to beguile him into music again. And after some days of fruitless exhortation on my part I hit upon a psychological deception that pried him from the somber, shuttered apartment and gave him the justification he required to remove to his lovely villa on Lago Maggiore. I pretended that I was feeling ill because of the intense heat in Milan. And when he suggested that I would feel better in his house on Lago Maggiore, I said that I had come to Milan not for my health, but to be with him. He had, therefore, no choice but to take me to Lago Maggiore. Some days after we had moved to the villa I hit upon another ruse that turned his thoughts to music. Sitting with him in his room, into which a Stein-way grand had been hopefully moved, I began to speak about Meyerbeer, and wondered whether he had ever heard the once-celebrated but now completely neglected opera *Robert le diable.* The Maestro replied, with a sud-den show of interest, that he had played it once as a cellist in the orchestra of a small theater in Italy more than half a century ago. "I suppose you don't remember any of it after so many years," I remarked with affected casualness. "I remember very well," he snapped, as if I had insulted him. And, sitting down at the piano, he began *Robert le diable* from the beginning and played and sang for a long time, imparting to the text the dramatic flavor of an actual performance. He had broken a two-month musical fast! And, watching his expressive face and eyes reflecting every shade of the words and music of the antiquated, forgotten opera, his three children, Walter, Wanda, and Wally, who were present, were overcome with emotion and had to turn away to hide their happy tears.

From that day he resumed his normal preoccupation with music. In the morning we heard him playing the piano. After lunch we sat on the terrace overlooking the lake. He would gaze silently at the water and then suddenly say something about a score that he had been going over in his mind. "There is something in *Ibéria* I do not understand. . . . You know, at the end of—" and he would run briskly up to his room and return with the Debussy score and point out the place and tell me that he was tempted to double the woodwinds there, but that perhaps it was his own fault, not Debussy's, and the next time he rehearsed *Ibéria* he would ask the orchestra to . . .

In the evening, after supper, we would all go up to his room, where his son had installed a powerful phonograph. I would pretend that we were all going to a concert and arrange a different program of his records for each night. The maid would bring bottles of red syrup and glasses on a tray. Fortified with drinks, we disposed ourselves around the phonograph and listened to his records for an hour and a half, exclaiming "Oh" and "Ah" rapturously (and sincerely) at certain moments, greatly to the old man's delight. He himself sat upright in a chair and conducted the music with the vigor and passion he displayed at rehearsals and performances. *"Accidente!"* (uncanny) he would exclaim admiringly, his right arm still beating time, his left pressing his side to indicate the warmth and insistence of a melody, as the orchestra executed some difficult or subtle passage. And when we said good-night and dispersed to our rooms, we would often be startled by the horrible scratch of a phonograph needle and an ensuing fortissimo blast of exaggerated orchestral sound, and would know that the Maestro, who was congenitally unable to cope with the simplest contraption, was braving the awesome, complicated machine in order to hear again a portion of a record he had either liked or disliked at the recent "concert." Or later, in the dead of night, if one slept lightly, one could hear from the direction of his room the faint, compressed sound of music from his short-wave radio, thus justifying his resentment of those who inquired, in all innocence, if he slept well, and bearing out his claim that in all his life he had slept hardly at all. I had also discounted his boast that he had never, for the reason that he disliked his face, looked at himself in a mirror, even while shaving; until, entering his room one morning, I found him sitting up in bed, wielding a safety razor and gazing unconcernedly the while at Lago Maggiore.

As I had promised the Maestro, I engaged the tenor he wanted for *Un Ballo in Maschera*. Although the opera was scheduled for late in the season, preparations for it were begun even before Toscanini arrived in New York in late September. As the time drew near for the broadcast, the usual troubles attendant upon an undertaking that involved singers descended on us. The artists had previous commitments to fill, and it was difficult to arrange even a tentative schedule of rehearsals. The Maestro could not, of course, comprehend any difficulties where he was concerned. As he gave himself up completely to the preparation of an opera, so he took it for granted that the vocalists, no matter how popular they might be and how much in demand for concert and operatic engagements elsewhere, would do the same and be at all times at his disposal. And on learning that they would not be, he flew into a rage and threatened to abandon the project altogether, leave America, and what not.

Such crises had been usual during his many years at NBC. By dint of pressure, cajoling, and manipulation of schedules, the difficulties had always been surmounted. And now, after a last-minute substitution of Jan Peerce for the indisposed Bjoerling, all matters were

ironed out and the day of the first rehearsal with Toscanini approached. Then, one morning, I was hastily summoned to the Maestro in Riverdale. I found him
slumped in a chair, his face tearstained. He embraced
me and clung to me pathetically. "If you are my friend,
as you say, you must save me," he pleaded. "I cannot
conduct. . . . I am too old. . . . I should have stopped last year with the *Missa Solemnis*. I must go away
and hide myself in a corner and die. This morning I
awo-ked and I cannot remember the words of *Ballo!* No
word can I remember! I cannot remember no*thing!* I
cannot face my artists so." "But you remember the
music?" I said hopefully. He pursed his lips contemptu-
ously. "The music? Yes, I remember the music . . .
but the words, *no!* I cannot look my artists in the face
without knowing the words. I cannot go on. Save me,
caro . . . let me go. . . ." I kissed his forehead and
assured him that his happiness and peace of mind were
my only concern. I would do as he asked. I would cancel
Ballo in Maschera and find another conductor to take
over the three or four broadcasts that remained of the
season. I left Riverdale thinking that it had come at last,
that all things must have an end. I telephoned a conductor who by chance was free to undertake the remaining broadcasts, and I set about canceling *Un Ballo*.

I had completed these sad arrangements when the
Maestro called me on the telephone one morning. He
was very excited. "*Pensa* [think], *caro*," he cried, "I
awake this morning and I remember *all* the words of

Ballo! I can now face my artists. Call the rehearsal. *Addio, caro!"* I telephoned the substitute conductor and the singers and countermanded the cancelation of the opera. At the orchestral rehearsal a day later Toscanini, smiling and in the best of humor, sang every word of the entire *Ballo in Maschera* with his familiar expressiveness, the while he guided the instrumentalists deftly and enthusiastically. The broadcast performance went off in great style. Afterward he entertained the members of the cast in a private room in a downtown restaurant. He beamed with satisfaction, professed himself not at all fatigued, and delighted his guests with old stories and anecdotes; and those of the singers who had a flair for mimicry amused him with take-offs of celebrated musicians, including some of himself.

But, notwithstanding this sudden remarkable resurgence of memory, it was clear to the Maestro's family and friends that the time had arrived for him to relinquish his broadcasts. In this the Maestro fully concurred, frowning on any suggestion that he return for another season. His son, Walter, at his father's request, prepared a letter of resignation addressed to Mr. Sarnoff and placed it on the Maestro's desk for his signature. But days and weeks passed and the letter lay unsigned, for the document had become a symbol of abdication to the old man. And it was not until the week of his final broadcast of the season that he summoned the resolution to put his name to it and send it off.

For his farewell broadcast he had arranged an all-

Wagner program, which included the Prelude and *Liebestod* from *Tristan und Isolde*. But at the first rehearsal he summoned me to his room and told me that he could no longer remember the music of *Tristan* and would play instead the Overture and Bacchanale from *Tannhäuser*, which, he said, he remembered quite well. I recalled his recent temporary crisis over *Ballo*, and I suggested that he might perhaps awake the following morning with the *Tristan* music clear in his mind. But he shook his head sadly and said he was certain that it would never come back to him. So the substitution was quickly arranged, and the next day he rehearsed the *Tannhäuser* with his usual power and subtlety. It occurred to me that a desire to prove to the public (and to himself) that he could summon the strength and endurance to prepare and conduct the long excerpt from *Tannhäuser*, with its powerful rhythms and tremendous sonorities, had actually brought about a temporary loss of memory for the less arduous music of *Tristan*. The *Tannhäuser* piece, followed by the brilliant *Meistersinger* Prelude for a finish, would enable him to wind up his career of nearly seventy years with an exhibition of undiminished vitality and with all his artistic faculties beautifully apparent. In effect, he would lay down his baton while still at the height of his powers.

My belief that he had, perhaps, unconsciously adopted this innocent stratagem was strengthened at the actual broadcast of his final concert. For he began the *Tannhäuser* Overture with his customary air of obsessive authority, arrived by inevitable gradation at the climax, and with controlled fury plunged into the maelstrom of the Bacchanale. Whatever anxieties his family and I had had up to his appearance on the stage were now completely routed. From behind the engineers in the control booth I watched at close range the powerful gyrations of his baton, the mystic behavior of his left hand, and the subtle conspiratorial expressions of his eyes and lips. The audience, as if aware of the significance of the occasion, stared at his head and back with frozen concentration, each person seemingly oblivious of his neighbor, like witnesses of some awesome and perilous event.

The frenzy of the Bacchanale gradually died down, the passion exhausted. The piece was nearing its end. At the point where the offstage strings faintly echo the turbulence of the orgiastic night and retreat ghostlike before the thin, uneasy dawn, Toscanini's stick wavered and began to describe unintelligible motions. The orchestra, suddenly frightened, followed for a few bars, through habit, their Maestro's curious, unrelated gestures. Then, instinctively assuming direction, the men tried desperately to coalesce and reach the end in unity, though without the finesse of leadership. The attempt, beset by self-consciousness and fear, was a failure. In the soft cacophony that ensued, the Maestro ceased conducting and put his hand to his eyes. The men stopped playing and the house was engulfed in terrible silence.

Perhaps only thirty seconds passed, but it was like

a year. Then the Maestro, like a Tannhäuser banishing with a gesture the miasma of the Venusberg, straightened up, lifted his baton for a powerful downbeat, and swung the men into the *Meistersinger* Prelude. Slightly unsteady, yet rhythmic and sonorous enough to be unmistakably Toscanini, the Prelude coursed along. Now it seemed that nothing untoward could occur. Then, at the very end, it happened. Toscanini's arm was seen to falter. It came down and rested, motionless, at his side. The baton slipped from his hand. He stepped unsteadily from the podium and walked with drooping head off-stage, while the orchestra behind him screamed out the exultant, throaty C Major jubilance of the Prelude's final bar. It sounded like the world's affirmative judgment on the man who had for so long revealed to it the naked marvel of great music. He was now, before their very eyes, stumbling toward silence, probably forever.

Or so it looked. One last commitment remained for Toscanini—to remake portions of the recordings of *Un Ballo* and *Aïda*. The session had been scheduled for the Wednesday after the Maestro's farewell broadcast. There could now be no question but that the session would be canceled. But on Monday, to our surprise, Toscanini sent word that he would be ready to record. And on Wednesday he arrived at Carnegie Hall, punctual as usual. He greeted everybody pleasantly and changed into his rehearsing coat. Shutting his eyes tightly and screwing up his face in a mock-painful expression, he sprinkled Eau de Cologne generously over head and face, wielding the atomizer with comic vigor. Then he walked rapidly down the long flight of stairs to the stage without touching the banister and quickly gained his podium. With his baton he rapped sharply on the music stand at his side. "*Andiamo*," he cried, and brought his right arm down in a powerful downbeat.

As if mesmerized, singers and orchestra sang and played with an artistry beyond their conscious abilities. And those who only listened marveled at the conductor's flagrant energy, his secure memory and uncanny synchronization of pose and gesture with the design and content of the music. Was it the upsetting ordeal of a public farewell to music which had, only three days before, disturbed for a few moments the fabulous memory, the superb control over his musical faculties, the easy mastery over his orchestra, all now so beautifully evident? The Toscanini who was now recording *Un Ballo* and *Aïda* was in all respects the autocratic, confident, extraordinary perfectionist the world had known for more than half a century.

A NOTE ON THE TYPE

This book was set on the Linotype in ELECTRA, *designed by W. A. Dwiggins. The Electra face is a simple and readable type suitable for printing books by present-day processes. It is not based on any historical model, and hence does not echo any particular time or fashion. It is without eccentricities to catch the eye and interfere with reading— in general, its aim is to perform the function of a good book printing-type: to be read, and not seen.*

The book was composed, printed, and bound by Kingsport Press, Inc., Kingsport, Tennessee. The paper was made by P. H. Glatfelter Co., Spring Grove, Pa. The typography and binding were designed by Charles E. Skaggs.